Finding Your
Blind Spots

8
**Guiding Principles
for Overcoming
Implicit Bias
in Teaching**

HEDREICH NICHOLS

Solution Tree | Press

a division of
Solution Tree

555 North Morton Street
Bloomington, IN 47404
800.733.6786 (toll free) / 812.336.7700
FAX: 812.336.7790

email: info@SolutionTree.com
SolutionTree.com

Visit **go.SolutionTree.com/diversityandequity** to download the free reproducibles in this book.

Printed in the United States of America

Library of Congress Cataloging-in-Publication Data

Names: Nichols, Hedreich, author.
Title: Finding your blind spots : eight guiding principles for overcoming
    implicit bias in teaching / Hedreich Nichols.
Description: Bloomington, IN : Solution Tree Press, [2021] | Includes
    bibliographical references and index.
Identifiers: LCCN 2021047296 (print) | LCCN 2021047297 (ebook) | ISBN
    9781952812538 (Paperback) | ISBN 9781952812545 (eBook)
Subjects: LCSH: Reflective teaching--United States. | Discrimination in
    education--United States. | Whites--United States--Attitudes. |
    Prejudices--Prevention.
Classification: LCC LB1025.3 .N535 2021 (print) | LCC LB1025.3 (ebook) |
    DDC 371.14/4--dc23/eng/20211106
LC record available at https://lccn.loc.gov/2021047296
LC ebook record available at https://lccn.loc.gov/2021047297

Solution Tree
Jeffrey C. Jones, CEO
Edmund M. Ackerman, President

Solution Tree Press
President and Publisher: Douglas M. Rife
Associate Publisher: Sarah Payne-Mills
Art Director: Rian Anderson
Managing Production Editor: Kendra Slayton
Editorial Director: Todd Brakke
Copy Chief: Jessi Finn
Production Editor: Miranda Addonizio
Content Development Specialist: Amy Rubenstein
Acquisitions Editor: Sarah Jubar
Copy Editor: Mark Hain
Proofreader: Sarah Ludwig
Text and Cover Designer: Kelsey Hergül
Editorial Assistants: Charlotte Jones, Sarah Ludwig, and Elijah Oates

For my son, my inspiration.

Acknowledgments

I would like to acknowledge Mervil Johnson, writer and award-winning community leader; Simone Gisler, researcher, writer, and multilingual educator from Switzerland; and Tia Luker-Putra, global educator and STEM, SDG, and DEI authority in Shanghai, for their estimable reviews and counsel. I would also like to acknowledge Sarah Jubar, for her vision and for connecting me to the Solution Tree family, and Dave Hennel for connecting me to everyone else.

Solution Tree Press would like to thank the following reviewers:

Nadya Bech-Conger
Instructional Coach
Hunt Middle School
Burlington, Vermont

Todd Bloch
Science Teacher
Warren Woods Middle School
Warren, Michigan

Erin Kruckenberg
Fifth-Grade Teacher
Jefferson Elementary School
Harvard, Illinois

Emily Terry
English Teacher
Kinard Middle School
Fort Collins, Colorado

Toby West
District Data Coordinator
Delaware City Schools
Delaware, Ohio

Visit **go.SolutionTree.com/diversityandequity** to download
the free reproducibles in this book.

Table of Contents

About the Author

 **Hedreich Nichols** is an author, educator, and founder of SmallBites Educational Consulting LLC. Through keynotes, workshops, and e-courses, Hedreich provides resources to help educators provide more student-centered experiences through equitable teaching practices. Hedreich has also authored five nonfiction books for middle school students as part of the Cherry Lake Publishing 21st Century Skills Library series that includes educator and student resources to drive conversations and learning around equity and belonging. To further help educators, Hedreich produces *SmallBites*, a vlog and podcast featuring vignettes and strategies to help educators become more inclusive and reflective practitioners, one small bite at a time.

Before getting her master's degree in education, Hedreich was a Grammy-nominated artist who traveled extensively, conducting music workshops and teaching historical empathy through the Black music experience. Her broad-based pedagogical experience in both well- and under-resourced settings gives Hedreich a unique perspective and a vision for helping educators build a cache of strategies that lead to better academic and social-emotional learning outcomes. In addition to working as an author, educator, and consultant, Hedreich works as the ed tech specialist on her district's curriculum and instructional team in North Texas, serves on the board of Sleeping Bear Press, and partners with organizations like Teach Better and InspireCitizens.org to further diversity, equity, and inclusion initiatives.

Hedreich received her master of education in educational technology from Texas A&M University and does her finest work as mom to her son, Christopher. He's her big why, and her hope is that the work she does will lead to better learning experiences and outcomes for kids who look like him.

To learn more about Hedreich's work, visit https://hedreich.com or follow her @ hedreich on Twitter and Hedreich Nichols on Instagram, Facebook, and LinkedIn.

To book Hedreich Nichols for professional development, contact pd@SolutionTree .com.

Foreword

By Walter D. Greason

Education requires faster and more effective adaptation from its professionals than any other field. Consider the relative stagnation in fields like accounting, engineering, or law. The principles and core practices have been established for a century, and changes in these fields are regularly scrutinized for a decade before institutional adoption. Even in dynamic areas like medicine, absent a major crisis, the standards of best practice remain largely stable. Education, on the other hand, requires constant reassessment of daily practice. Individual students require specific engagement and intervention to help them learn the most from one class to another. Those needs vary constantly and in unpredictable ways. While many imagine the classroom as a site of scientific expertise and precision, it is, in fact, an art gallery where creativity and spontaneity carry as much power as evidence and methodology.

No educator better embodies this changing balance, and the agility necessary to maintain it, than Hedreich Nichols. Her dedication to innovation and accountability with the success of both students and teachers at the center of their collaborative work is unmatched. Raising questions about the most pressing issues in education worldwide while simultaneously developing new solutions that empower interactive learning, teaching, and research, Nichols has emerged as one of the most important voices in leading educational content development in the world.

Every day, and all day long, Nichols shares breakthroughs in advanced instructional practices. Her voice keeps the community of learners grounded in a shared commitment to the wellness and aspirations of every classroom participant. In *Finding Your Blind Spots*, she offers a blueprint to answering the challenges presented in works like Ibram X. Kendi's (2019) *How to Be an Antiracist*. Kendi (2019) provides a framework and governing principles to make belonging a priority in every classroom and school. Nichols goes further by specifying techniques and interventions that counter the traditions of educational exclusion that remain far too common in the United States and worldwide.

Finding Your Blind Spots marks the emergence of a new day in global education in which educators have the resources and reach to share the most impactful techniques for students and their families. I am a proud member of Hedreich Nichols's peer learning network, and I urge every teacher and educator to consider her insights about the teaching and learning processes.

Introduction

If you are reading this, my assumption is that you are a K–12 educator or administrator looking for tools and strategies to help you better reach and teach your students. Your school demographic may be different from the demographic of the neighborhood where you grew up. It may look different from the neighborhood you live in now. Your school may look much different than the circle of family and friends who generally share and reinforce your thoughts and beliefs. The children and young adults in your classrooms may look different from the students in classrooms of the past. Your students may espouse notions on culture, religion, politics, gender, and justice that are very different from yours. That may be something you find amazing; it may be something you find enlightening but challenging. It may be something that, in a quiet corner of your mind, you find alarming. Whatever you feel about diversity, it's OK. The fact that you are here, reading this book, says that you have a desire to uncover any blind spots, build bridges, foster better relationships, and have a more inclusive school community.

My Recurring Role as an OBF

Starting school early in Houston Independent School District's mass desegregation history put me on track to becoming a recurring OBF—that is, a one Black friend. It was the 1970s in Texas, and not everybody was happy about the mixing of the races. I was usually the only Black student in class, and I experienced my share of name-calling and microaggressions. But mostly, I passed through primary school as a "credit to my race," the affable Black girl who skipped a grade and could sing. I was well behaved, "well spoken," and had all the "codes of power" a Black person needed to be successful in a White world (White & Ali-Khan, 2013).

Those *codes of power*, which are the unwritten rules and sociolinguistic norms of the dominant culture, allowed me to learn things as an OBF that I didn't know I was learning, unknowingly storing them up for use in my own journey as an educator and author. I will share those lessons with you, and more, in the form of practical strategies and actionable steps to help you:

- Discover any blind spots or biases you might have

- Mitigate any unwanted influence and fallout from those blind spots and biases

- Guide you toward more inclusivity in your classroom and on your campus

While I am writing this as everybody's OBF, I am not the sole expert on Blackness, minority-ness, female-ness, or any of the other-nesses. I can't give blanket advice on how to reach and understand all minority students, not even all Black female students. What I can do is provide you with knowledge and strategies to help you engage all learners, especially students who may lack a strong sense of belonging in your school community.

Many of the things you'll learn in this book are simply instructional best practice, and I hope you will find that you are already a reflective practitioner doing a lot of things right. Other parts of the book will help you build a bridge of inclusivity for students whose ideas, motivations, and actions you may have more difficulty understanding. The one thing this book doesn't do is pass judgment. Having bias is natural, not a trait that puts humans into good and evil categories. It's not only natural—it's necessary. Imagine if your brain fully considered each bit of information you took in. The cognitive load would be unmanageable. Bias is an outgrowth of being able to immediately sort the daily influx of data into immediately recognizable categories (see figure I.1).

Figure I.1: Categorizing data in recognizable ways.

One of the categories we form early on is *us*. Most children naturally begin with *mama*, and from there they sort the world around them into categories: family, neighborhood, team, country, and so on. The familiar, the *usses*, draws a circle around those people and things we innately trust. Drawing a distinction between *us* and *them* is an "unavoidable fact of life" (Luhmann, 1988, p. 95). People instinctively trust the familiar and distrust what is new or unfamiliar.

The positive bias that people feel toward the familiar is not a bad thing—until it is. *Positive bias* is the natural tendency to like certain things and people—often the familiar—and to distrust other, often lesser-known entities. It's uncomfortable to admit that our bias may have grown into prejudice, racism, misogyny, and so on that disadvantages others, but it happens. In our classrooms, for instance, it's common to come up with bias-based concepts about different types of students, even archetypes that go beyond race or gender identity: the "jock," the "mean girl," the "rapper," the "drama queen," the "nerd," and so on. In thinking about your classes, you could no doubt ascribe some of these labels to some of your students. This book will give you the knowledge and skills to identify the places of bias that adversely affect your practice and give you strategies to move beyond those biases to build a more equitable, inclusive campus culture. This book won't be difficult to read, but it may be hard to digest. Still, by thinking, feeling, reflecting, and learning your way through these pages, you will come to embrace yourself and your students in a way that will transform your school community into a more welcoming place for all.

Book Overview

In the chapters of this book, you will learn to explore your classrooms and campuses through the eyes of an *other*, a person who society at large or an in-group views as an outlier, an outsider, one of *them* rather than one of *us*. The lessons I have learned as an other, both sitting in and standing in front of school desks, I share with you in the hope that you will use the humor, pain, incredulity, and even mundanity of those lessons to become a better-prepared, more inclusive educator. Those experiences, combined with extensive research, are woven together into an educational framework of eight guiding principles that will provide you with insight into the educational experience of students who do not belong to the mainstream, dominant culture. These principles will arm you with social-emotional and teaching strategies to help you better understand and educate students who might look, dress, or identify in a way that you may find difficult to decode.

In chapter 1, you will examine your own bias and learn about the adverse impact it can have on student achievement. In chapter 2, you will analyze guilt as an impetus for change, but eschew it as a paralyzing force or grounds for giving your students less rigorous learning experiences. In chapter 3, you will learn how language choices can subtly reinforce racism, sexism, ableism, and other forms of discrimination, as well as how these choices can impact your students' sense of self, their academic progress, and even their economic future. After learning to choose your words more empathetically, you will move on to making curriculum changes to include diverse perspectives and stories in chapter 4, exploring the impact of intentionality in making curriculum and library choices that reflect a more varied cultural community. In chapter 5, you will investigate the subtleties of cultural acceptance and rejection, and you will also learn that language style and intelligence are not intrinsically linked. In chapter 6, you will explore gender, sexuality, and identity while developing strategies for supporting students and families from the lesbian, gay, bisexual, transgender, and queer or questioning (LGBTQ+) community. In chapter 7, you'll identify ways to celebrate diversity daily, and in chapter 8, you'll be able to dissect and recognize microaggressions that can prevent educators from building the relationships they hope to foster. In chapter 8, you'll also learn to (hopefully) avoid some common faux pas when interacting with students from cultural groups that may be less familiar to you.

In this book, you will explore all the tools you need to move from checking a *celebrate diversity* box during heritage months to fostering a deep sense of inclusivity and belonging for students who, because of race, gender, religion, sexuality, or perhaps more individual reasons, feel that they are *them* and not *us*. At the end of each chapter, you will find a section, Reflection to Action, that's designed to help you use what you've learned in the chapter to reflect on what you still need to work on, your personal growth, and how you can put what you are learning into action. Then, when you are ready, try the activities in the tables throughout the book with the group or groups you work with. Doing so will not only help you stay accountable but also give those around you the chance to reflect on their beliefs and blind spots as well.

Finding Your Blind Spots is not just another book about culturally responsive teaching. It's an experiential learning handbook written by an educator for educators, based on academic research and lived experience as both a student and teacher from a nondominant culture. It's a book you can use a chapter at a time or in its entirety as a book study or campus guide. It's a book you can refer to time and again because the strategies can be referenced in cycles. As culture norms shift in your learning community and as your perception and acceptance of those shifts evolve, you can circle back to chapters in the book to rediscover and implement bits of knowledge you may not have been able to use at first reading.

Spoiler alert: this book will not stop you from gathering information about the people around you and recognizing archetypes. The guy in the letter jacket with the outgoing personality may indeed be the quarterback. The girl with the black army boots, heavy black eyeliner, and blue hair may indeed love her SoundCloud emo playlist. Those kinds of cues might provide you with relationship and conversation starters. As much as we want to see people as blank slates, it's not possible or even necessary. Colorblindness does not exist, and celebrating cultural and group identity is a good thing. But identity within a group is only one part of who your students are, so it's important to see archetypes without allowing yourself to stereotype or pigeonhole your students. Seeing them as one-dimensional cultural caricatures prevents educators from examining "the operation of implicit bias, racial anxiety, and stereotype threat" that so often hinders the success of students who aren't born into the dominant culture (Godsil, Tropp, Goff, & Powell, 2014, p. 4). Wanting your classroom and campus to be truly inclusive requires that you are intentional in building and supporting relationships. It doesn't require compromising your values, but it may require a shift in thinking that allows you to teach more and judge less.

I would recommend using a journal and taking notes while reading the chapters of this book. Many of the questions and ideas will require more than passing thought, and as you continue to learn, at some point you will want to look back and see how far you've come. Let's begin.

CHAPTER ONE

Bias and Belonging

My life as an other started early. I was an avid reader in kindergarten, which meant I was bored and often in trouble for "helping." I would offer to identify all the letters, pronounce all the words, and help my classmates by completing their early literacy tasks for them, since sitting quietly after completing my own work was not my strong suit; the teacher found this disruptive. That carried on another year or so. Then, after skipping a grade in a newly integrated school, I was both the youngest in class and the only Black person in the room, which became a recurring norm. I made good grades but was forgetful and not particularly organized. These days, a diverse learner like me gets some letters in a medical record, but this was before attention deficit hyperactivity disorder (ADHD), twice exceptional (2e gifted) learning differences, or any other types of neurodiversity were recognized. On top of it all, I am an only child, bookish, and gifted in music and drama—so in short, a poster child for other. I am fortunate to always find my people, but I know well the joys—and pains—of not being able to find the box, much less get inside it. I know a lot about what it's like to be *them*, rather than *us*.

In some ways, this is the most important chapter in the book, the first step toward creating more inclusive classrooms, campuses, and communities. In recognizing personal blind spots and mitigating personal bias, this chapter lays a foundation not only for the other chapters in this book but also for how you approach your learning objectives and implementation goals as you become a better teacher for all your students. This chapter is the first step on your journey. As with every problem-based learning framework, the eight guiding principles are a cycle, moving you through empathy and ideation to demonstration before leading you to a point of reflection and evaluation that inevitably draws you back into the process. This cycle gives you ample opportunity to deepen your learning by retracing your steps, making tweaks and adaptations along the way (see figure 1.1, page 8).

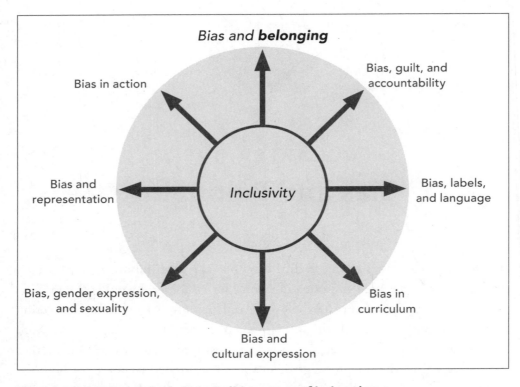

Figure 1.1: Guiding principle 1—Build a sense of belonging.

As stated in this book's introduction, creating a circle of trust, your *usses*, is natural. Your circle of trust includes *your* parents, *your* family, *your* neighborhood, *your* place of worship, folks who look like you, folks who think like you, folks who speak the same language as you, or come from your college, city, or country: people who *get* you. All those things make up the identity around which people separate their *usses* from their *thems*. However, with the exception of family, none of those identity markers are biological concepts. That type of natural trust and inclusion is called *affinity bias*, which is the unconscious inclination to gravitate to and connect with those who are like us. And while it is natural, it can also be harmful to others, causing people to unconsciously disenfranchise those they perceive as different. Affinity bias is one of 175 cognitive biases identified by researcher and professor Hershey H. Friedman (2017) of Brooklyn College in his collected research from diverse sources on what he calls *cognitive shortcuts*. His use of work from the U.S. military and CIA comes closest to explaining why it is important to "identify the simplifying rules of thumb that people use to make judgments on incomplete or ambiguous information" (Heuer, 2008, as cited in Friedman, 2017, p. 4).

When affinity bias, or any other cognitive bias, works to the detriment of others, it's called implicit or hidden bias. *Implicit bias* is when people's natural affinity is for those who are like them. Sometimes, this has negative consequences for those unlike them. This usually happens when we find ourselves confronted with a reality that is incongruent with our beliefs about that reality. This dissonance can cause us to unintentionally disenfranchise others. For example, imagine that five male students walk into Advanced Placement (AP) algebra class wearing school team gear and carrying basketballs. A teacher might immediately point them in the direction of the regular mathematics class down the hall. This is because athletes, especially male athletes, are often depicted as students who struggle academically. The reality of five athletes in AP mathematics is incongruent with this teacher's picture of the typical AP student; she's experiencing cognitive dissonance. Alternately, if the five boys were known to be last year's science fair winners, they would probably be welcomed in without much ado. In either situation, the teacher would not be displaying an intentional bias. Yet, such a reaction affects how a teacher welcomes—or does not welcome—students.

Intentional Consonance, Unintentional Dissonance

If people's constructs of who they are have more to do with what they feel most familiar with, then people can change to create more inclusive circles of trust. The key is to become aware of the unintentional ways that bias can manifest and to be more intentional about those thoughts and feelings. Cognitive biases cause us to make judgments without having all the information, and it happens unintentionally. Researchers have found that "the brain seeks simplicity and it does so by categorizing people and things in order to more easily and instantaneously assess how those people or things compare to or affect us"; further, we are "biochemically disposed" to think empathetically about others like us because it mirrors the generosity we extend to ourselves (Davis, 2020). While the science behind bias may make overcoming it sound like a daunting task, like any other life change, it begins with the acknowledgement that something is amiss and a desire to be better.

The Kirwan Institute for the Study of Race and Ethnicity (2012) at Ohio State University says that biases are malleable and that "the implicit associations that we have formed can be gradually unlearned through a variety of debiasing techniques." Debiasing techniques can range from awareness trainings to video game simulations. They all have the goal of raising your awareness so that you can base decisions on more complete information and take fewer cognitive shortcuts. As a matter of fact, by reading this chapter and reflecting on your biases, you are already utilizing one type of debiasing technique.

Just as the separation anxiety and stranger danger of childhood give way to more inclusive forms of socialization as you grow, you can unlearn bias and learn new ways of relating to the unfamiliar. *Negative bias*, the kind of bias that can adversely affect the way you relate to others, tends to be stronger than positive messaging (Liebrecht, Hustinx, & van Mulken, 2019), so confronting and weeding out bias is a must for teachers, and it's doable. Figure 1.2, adapted from the work of Anuj Jain (2019) on bias and fairness in artificial intelligence, provides a visual representation of types of negative and positive bias and how those biases can play out in real-world situations.

In all of the interactions in these examples, we recognize two-legged creatures. This is how bias helps us sort information in a way that is necessary. We can distinguish a bear from a human: an immediately threatening wild animal is different from a student on a field trip. However, when our biases affect how we perceive threat, beauty, or good and bad ideologies, those biases and underlying associations can go from being positive to negative. A good way to start the process of becoming more intentional about this thinking is to consider how your brain categorizes people.

Who are your others? How are they different from each other? How are they different from you? Were you once a popular athlete who now has difficulty relating to the science fair–winning student who doesn't like to make eye contact? Are you the educated child or grandchild of immigrants who has a difficult time relating to students with working-class parents who may not speak English well? Are you a conservative Christian who has difficulty relating to nontraditional expressions of gender? Perhaps you are an inclusive educator who has a hard time with teachers or students you see expressing prejudice toward certain groups.

None of these are human conditions that need healing. However, in certain professions, bias has far-reaching impact: judges who sentence Black male offenders to longer sentences than similarly situated White male offenders (United States Sentencing Commission, n.d.); doctors who have higher infant mortality rates in the Black community (Kirby, 2017); science, technology, engineering, and mathematics (STEM) human resources professionals who are less likely to hire women and minorities (Graf, Fry, & Funk, 2018); and educators who are more likely to refer Black and brown students to the office for disciplinary reasons (Welsh & Little, 2018) than to gifted and AP programs (Grissom & Redding, 2016).

The end effect of bias and poor teacher-student relationships is not small. What begins as unintentional bias in the classroom ends up contributing to the social-emotional wellness and indeed the success or failure of whole communities. Researchers Travis Riddle and Stacey Sinclair's (2019) studies cite various statistics and metrics that show how bias contributes to the structural racism that continues to negatively impact the education, and ultimately the economics, of diverse populations:

Bias Type

ETHICAL ←—————————————————→ UNETHICAL

Intentional (Good to have)	Unintentional (Good to avoid)	Unintentional (Avoid)	Intentional (Prevent)
Biases are an outgrowth of normal cognitive functioning and helpful in sorting and filtering information.	Biases may unconsciously influence judgment or decision making.	Interactions and reactions are based on unconscious, preconceived ideas and beliefs.	Biases are intentionally used to belittle or disenfranchise others.
Example: The two-legged creature just off the trail is a bear and not one of the students on a field trip. The bear represents danger; the teacher needs to act quickly and keep everyone safe.	Example: The two-legged creature in the classroom is a large man who is angry and seems threatening. Something seems off, and he does not have a visitor's badge, so the teacher calmly and firmly directs him to the office.	Example: The two-legged creature on the dance team is a fourteen-year-old girl who wears a large afro. The teacher asks her if she can straighten and tame her hair so that she fits in with the other girls who wear long, flowing hair.	Example: The two-legged creature in the collaborative team meeting is a teacher who made a statement during team huddle that appears incongruent with the ideological opinions of most of the staff at the school. She receives a terse email telling her to keep politics out of staff discussions, even though other staff members are readily allowed to express their opinions.
These biases are necessary and do not impact the way we perceive or interact with people.	While the perception of threat may or may not stem from bias, directing the person to the office is standard protocol and is a fair outcome. Reflecting on whether the perception of threat was based in bias would be a good next step.	While the dance team look may have been based on European standards of beauty in the past, recognizing that Afrocentric hair should not have to be "tamed" to look neat or attractive is an important step in normalizing diverse standards of beauty.	The rule allowing some opinions to be openly given should apply to all opinions, not just popularly held ones. Working toward creating a team culture that welcomes diverse ideologies and opinions would be a good next step.

Source: Adapted from Jain, 2019.

Figure 1.2: Types of bias and their impact on fairness.

> For example, if teachers and administrators are biased, then they may be more likely to make decisions that are unfavorable to black students, such as deciding that a given misbehavior is worthy of disciplinary action. Similarly, if members of the community are biased, they may more readily perceive transgressions from black students than from white students. The consequences of such interactions may be especially likely to lead to disparate outcomes.

When seen through the lens of the sound social-emotional, academic, and economic future that most people strive for, educators' personal biases can do lasting harm to the students they encounter. Even biases that grow out of a good place can damage campus culture. For example, not wanting to push students too hard may mean that teachers minimize rigor in learning experiences and could underscore the belief that the work may be too difficult for certain populations. Alternately, working hard to show the lone nonbinary student in your class that you are OK with the LGBTQ+ community by reminding them repeatedly that they are OK with you can actually come off as inauthentic.

Exploring the biases in oneself begins with critical self-reflection and emotional intelligence (EI), which the following sections cover. Critical self-reflection is important to confronting our flaws and weaknesses, and EI is a key way to bolster the ability to do this successfully and constructively while navigating interpersonal relationships.

Critical Self-Reflection

Here you might expect research or book recommendations, but the first step to creating more inclusive classrooms is less about external learning and more about getting to know yourself better. Learning about how you *other* is learning about yourself. Being knowledgeable on how othering and bias work will not make you a more inclusive educator; knowing how you other and becoming aware of—and mitigating—your own biases will. These reflections should not lead you to feel burdened by remorse or guilt, but they should free you to become a better educator and citizen.

You can change up your curriculum, add diverse books to your library, and find the most appealing dolls and puzzles for your centers that include all kinds of people. But if you don't change *you*, it'll be like forgetting to put salt in the soup. The best ingredients cannot replace salt, and you are the salt. Your students need more than the right learning materials. They need to connect with you, an authentic educator who believes in them, who genuinely respects and hopefully likes them.

Critical self-reflection is the first step to creating a more inclusive environment for all your students. It's your "Start here." Before going further, commit to reflecting on your own personal biases and to being honest with yourself about how much you need to let go of. It's probably more than you think; many seemingly harmless thoughts end up being the very microaggressions that fuel systemic discrimination (we'll discuss microaggressions in much further detail in chapter 8, page 113). Using the emotional intelligence tool in the next section will help you begin this process.

Emotional Intelligence

Cultivating *emotional intelligence* (n.d.), "the capacity to be aware of, control, and express one's emotions, and to handle interpersonal relationships judiciously and empathetically," is one way to retrain our brains to be mindful of the impact emotions have on perceptions and decisions. One big part of EI is empathy. According to Janice Gassam (2020), author of *Dirty Diversity: A Practical Guide to Foster an Equitable and Inclusive Workplace for All*, empathy can be developed. Her book is written for corporate America, but her diversity, equity, and inclusion (DEI) strategies are useful for the education sector as well. Gassam (2020) recommends making empathy a metric for hiring and job performance as well as coaching staff on how to develop their capacity for empathy. One important tactic for developing empathy, according to Gassam (2020), is learning to slow down and really listen to gain understanding.

Most educators want the best for their students, but a lack of empathy or understanding might cause an incongruence between the goals an educator has for a student and the challenges presented by personal beliefs about that student. For example, if a heavier student wants to try out for the cheerleading squad, a teacher might suggest band or flag corps instead, thinking that the student's weight might prevent her from being chosen. Without knowing the student's talents, in this scenario, the teacher's dissuasion likely stems from certain beliefs about what a cheerleader "should" look like.

Knowing that it is not your intent to do harm, what can you do? How can you uncover hidden bias? How can you become more empathetic? How can you decide if you have work to do or how much work you have to do? Reflect on and answer the questions in figure 1.3 (page 14) to give yourself a sense of some of your feelings about gender and race. Feel free to make notes on your reflections to help you acknowledge your feelings and develop your emotional intelligence. Remember as you reflect, there are no right or wrong answers. Consider this reflection a temperature check for you and you alone.

Questions	Answers
Not including family, think of the three people closest to you. Are they culturally similar to you? Do they espouse the same religion and politics?	
How often do you use color as a descriptor, especially when describing those who don't look like you?	
Have you ever made "innocent" generalizations (asking a Black student to rap or assuming a pretty girl isn't qualified for the science fair)?	
Have you ever used gender or sexuality in a derogatory way ("Oh, that's so gay"; "You throw like a girl")?	

Figure 1.3: Reflection questions on gender and race.

*Visit **go.SolutionTree.com/diversityandequity** for a free reproducible version of this figure.*

I'll reiterate—there are no right or wrong answers, only answers to let you know how much work there is to do, and every one of us has some work to do. Go back and read over your answers thoughtfully. You may feel a little ashamed of some of your answers, or at least a little sheepish, and that's OK. Or, you may be wondering what the fuss is all about. If you are, that's OK too. "You throw like a girl" is so common that you may not even notice that it's insulting both to the thrower and to women, many of whom throw better than some men. And who hasn't heard Dirk Nowitzki described as "that White dude who plays for the Mavericks"? Using any of the aforementioned comments, implying that someone doesn't belong or is an outlier, should not make you feel guilt, shame, or any other negative emotion. You don't need absolution; you just need to work on recognizing your blind spots. As I'll explore in chapter 2 (page 19), guilt or shame are not conducive to forward motion, and you want to move forward. Use the information you've gathered about yourself to cultivate emotional intelligence in your quest to become a more inclusive educator.

Before going to the next section, take out your journal and write down any notes or highlights from the chapter, as well as any personal calls to action you choose to set for yourself. Then, move on to the Reflection to Action section.

Exploring Your Implicit Bias

Here are two good places to start on your journey to understanding implicit bias.

1. **"Test Yourself for Hidden Bias" article:** Learning for Justice (http://learningforjustice.org), formerly Teaching Tolerance, is a must-have resource for educators working toward creating more classroom and campus inclusivity. The professional development article "Test Yourself for Hidden Bias" (https://bit.ly/3ifrJg3; Learning for Justice, n.d.) breaks down the logarithm of bias and links to Project Implicit's (n.d.) implicit association test (IAT) from Harvard, University of Virginia, and University of Washington psychologists.

   Since this IAT is a game rather than a standard question-and-answer format, it is very engaging and allows you to uncover hidden bias in a low-pressure format. Project Implicit offers a diverse selection of bias tests on different types of bias against various populations.

2. **LoveHasNoLabels.com:** Love Has No Labels (n.d.), "a movement to promote diversity, equity and inclusion of all people across race, religion, gender, sexual orientation, age and ability," similarly builds on personal reflection and personal hidden bias discovery as stepping-stones to action. Love Has No Labels also has small bites of information that connect to action steps. These action steps get you quickly moving toward change and better inclusivity. One best practice action step is the conversation starter (https://lovehasnolabels.com/onesmallstep) that helps you appropriately relate to people who are different from you so that you can engage with a broader group within your community. For some, talking to different kinds of people might be a matter of fact. For those raised and circulating in a homogenous circle, having conversations with people who are different might be awkward. Overcoming that awkwardness is one way to move from reflection to action.

Reflection to Action

Now that you have your journal ready, go through the following questions and answer them thoughtfully and honestly. If you feel the need to put a lock on your journal or type in a protected file, do that. These notes should be private so that you feel completely comfortable being transparent. This should also be the place that you give yourself grace and permission to be flawed, as we all are.

1. What did you learn from your implicit bias test?

2. Was the outcome what you expected? Why or why not?

3. Based on what you learned, what is one thing you want to work on specifically?

4. What are three ways you can use what you learned about yourself to better your practice *this week?*

Now that you have done the difficult work of critical self-reflection, it's time to choose a goal that impacts your learning or even personal community. The activities in table 1.1 will give you some ideas about where and how to begin.

Table 1.1: Sharing What I've Learned About Building a Sense of Belonging

Group	Activity
Littles (preK–grade 3)	Provide students with a crayon set that includes a variety of skin tones and shades, and have them do portraits of each other. Give students words to compare and contrast different attributes related to hair (*brunette, braided, afro, blonde, natural, straight, curly*), size (*taller, shorter, bigger, smaller*), and skin (*beige, rosy, tan, peach, caramel, chocolate, dark brown*). Contrast diverse physical attributes with things students have in common, like school, parents, teachers, love for ice cream, and so on.
Middles (grades 4–7)	Talk about the word *discrimination* and ask why students form groups that shut some students out. Ask students if their friends are more similar to them or more diverse. Talk about the whys behind their answers and why it's important to interact with all kinds of people. Have them come up with an action plan to diversify their groups. Ask students to think about generalizations like "boys love sports," or "girls love pink," and have them bring up their own. Discuss how generalizations can be harmful to groups and communities.

Group	Activity
Secondary	Ask students to think about generalizations and "in-groups." Ask them to discuss how those groups are formed and to consider whether or not they have value.
	Have students take the IAT on page 15 and discuss the results in as much or as little personal detail as you deem appropriate. Have them come up with action plans to correct their biases.
Staff	Have staff take the IAT and discuss the results in as much or as little personal detail as you deem appropriate. Have them come up with action plans to mitigate their biases.
	Ask teachers to reflect on their personal circles. If their circles are not diverse, ask them to reflect on how this might affect their educational practice.
Parents and Community	Explain to parents that your school wants to be a safe place for all students. Explain that it is important that all stakeholders consider their biases and treatment of others in order to make the world more welcoming for everyone. Consider having a culture corner in your newsletter—a short section that might include a fun fact about a particular culture, a recipe from a parent, or a greeting in another language. Consider regularly sharing links or reflection questions, like those in this chapter, in your newsletter.

CHAPTER TWO

Bias, Guilt, and Accountability

Guilt comes in many forms. Guilt is the reason we drag three small kids and a dog to both sets of grandparents' homes every Christmas instead of having the grandparents visit us. Guilt is the reason we receive a present after the fight we have when our partner forgets the anniversary of the day we met. Guilt is the reason for the heart-wrenching inadequacy educators feel balancing time spent on their school kids versus the time they spend with their own kids. There is survivor guilt, natural guilt, false guilt, and a long list of psychologically termed types of guilt. There is so much guilt, and there is so little use for it.

I was raised in a fairly conservative Christian community in the Bible Belt, and *guilt is from the devil* was a commonly used phrase. As I matured, I often remembered that phrase, in stark contrast to the sermons that seemed often to revolve around guilt. Toxic shame and guilt about one misstep or another were all too often preached to the exclusion of grace and forgiveness. I'll never forget sitting in church as a preteen, watching a crying, unmarried pregnant girl stand alone before the church to ask forgiveness. While I didn't have the words then to describe all the ways that was wrong, I knew that it was wrong.

When you begin to reflect and uncover your own biases, you may feel a tinge—or more than a tinge—of guilt for the way you've handled things up till now. Sometimes, viewing yourself and your human interactions critically is painful. Sometimes, the change that accompanies those reflections is painful. That pain is enough to heal from; you don't need to add the extra burden of guilt. Just as the young girl in my anecdote already felt the pain and ramifications of her situation and did not need to experience her pain and guilt publicly, you also don't need a spotlight shone on your own guilty feelings that might arise.

This chapter explores the role guilt plays in our unwillingness to face uncomfortable truths and how, in trading guilt for accountability, we can more readily address our biases and blind spots in order to become more empathetic and inclusive educators (see figure 2.1).

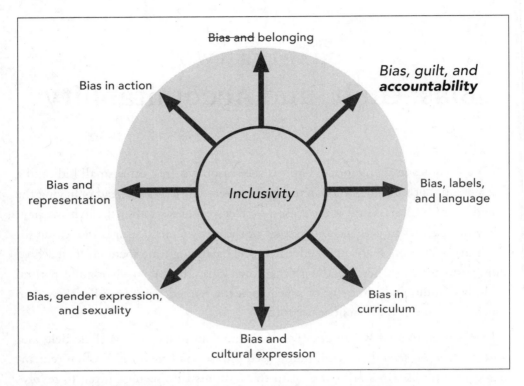

Figure 2.1: Guiding principle 2—Trade guilt for accountability.

In order to work through your feelings of guilt, it's important to recognize how these feelings can actually harm your students by keeping you from addressing your biases. This chapter will build your capacity to explore your personal bias in a way that builds your sense of accountability and motivates you to action. It will also help you discover ways to inspire and motivate others without being judgmental or off-putting.

Bad Guilt and Low Expectations

In the early 20th century, the Thomas theorem, a sociological theory developed by William Isaac Thomas and Dorothy Swaine Thomas (1928), recognized that students often lived out the reality the adults around them projected. When guilt, in the often inadvertent guise of sympathy, causes educators to coddle and indulge students, education scholars Daniel D. Liou, Tyson E. J. Marsh, and Rene Antrop-Gonzalez (2016) explain that low expectations "can dictate acceptable behaviors for achievement, and result in real consequences for the students." When your empathy becomes sympathy, you are less likely to provide the structure and rigor students need to develop the tenacity and tools for success in the face of real systemic hurdles. Neel Burton (2020), author of *Heaven and Hell: The Psychology of the Emotions*, summarizes sympathy as *I care about your suffering* and empathy as *I feel your suffering*. Empathy is understanding that a student might, for example, find herself in a tumultuous home situation. A teacher who empathizes makes sure that student has a counselor referral but also pushes her to get her assignments done, knowing that ultimately education will make a difference for her. Noah De Lissovoy (2008), professor in the department of curriculum and instruction at the University of Texas at Austin and author of *Power, Crisis, and Education for Liberation*, notes that when educators fail to prepare their students because they don't want to make a difficult home, economic, or family situation more difficult, they end up reinforcing the status quo. Far from helping, that can actually harm students. A teacher who sympathizes may be so concerned for the "poor child" that she gives the student a pass on important assignments instead of giving her the support she needs to push through difficult times. The teacher who sympathizes is subtly but unmistakably conveying the message that she believes the student's circumstances are bigger than her ability to overcome them.

If you have students who are in need, of course you should make sure that they get beneficial help and services. Teaching is always "Maslow before Bloom": meet psychological needs according to psychologist Abraham Maslow's (1987) hierarchy of needs (which was based on his work with the Siksika [Blackfoot] Nation in 1938; Baskin, 2002; Blackstock, 2011) before meeting academic needs explored in psychologist Benjamin Bloom's (1956) taxonomy. But. Low expectations—reducing assignment rigor, applying the rubric more benevolently, or allowing behavioral leeway—should not be the norm. Figure 2.2 (page 22) shows choices that take care of a student's needs versus choices that seem helpful but in actuality convey the message of low expectations.

There are of course real hardships that dictate real exceptions, but these should be outliers. Students suffering traumatic events like the loss of a close family member or violence in the home might need some leeway as they navigate the emotional and logistical demands of the crisis. Likewise, students dealing with sudden life changes, like finding out about a divorce or a parent's serious illness, may need a few extra days on major assignments or a retest as they regroup. In these cases, a counselor can help you strike a good balance between meeting academic and social-emotional

"Maslow Before Bloom" Choices	Low-Expectation Choices
Having healthy snacks or hygiene supplies discreetly available for students in need	Recommending that an unhoused student automatically sit out the unit test
Giving a student extra encouragement, including tutoring, in preparation for an AP test	Telling a student not to take on the added stress of AP classes
Allowing a student to have a cooling-off period after an outburst before assigning a consequence	Allowing a student to have frequent outbursts without consequences

Figure 2.2: Empathy-driven versus guilt-driven actions.

needs. As a teacher, you are of course sympathetic to the plight of your students, but your goal as an educator is to make sure that they are prepared academically for the future, even while they navigate difficult situations. As you expand your ability to better reach diverse students, remember that the opposite of good intent is often not bad intent but rather well-meant intent.

Discomfort Versus Shame

Outside the church doors, there's another kind of shaming going on. Well-known books and research articles on antiracism explore "White guilt" and "White fragility." *White guilt* is defined by psychologist Adam Rodriguez (n.d.) as "an individual or collective feeling of responsibility and ensuing guilt by a white person for harm resulting from the effects of current and historic racism." In the same article, Rodriguez references Robin DiAngelo (2011), author of "White Fragility," who describes *White fragility* as "a state in which even a minimum amount of racial stress becomes intolerable, triggering a range of defensive moves" (as cited in Rodriguez, n.d.).

These terms are valid, if uncomfortable, descriptors of ranges of reactions. They are not and should not be terms used to shame people into doing better. Learning about those topics and exploring them in relation to personal bias is valid and helpful, but it is also, let me emphasize, *personal*. The only standing up you need to do as you explore your comfort level with race, gender, sexuality, belief systems, and so on, is to stand up for students who need your support. Confession is optional, and no one has to give you absolution.

Keep Moving Forward

Exploring your level of comfort or burgeoning sense of culpability in your tacit support of systems that disenfranchise some populations should not keep you bound overlong to exploration and conversation. When you uncover your biases and explore any feelings that arise, the deep dive into your personal motivations can keep you stuck in the reflection phase instead of moving you toward focusing on turning empathy to action.

That's not to say that personal reflection will not be unsettling. Taking stock of your level of personal bias and othering patterns can take an emotional toll. Discomfort is normal; it's a sign that something needs to change, like getting overheated when you have on too many layers in a warm room. Guilt is also normal when you feel like you are a part of something that has caused someone harm. Moral guilt, for instance, is considered prosocial and can be an impetus for change. Shame, on the other hand, is considered an ugly, antisocial emotion and, according to psychology scholars Maria Miceli and Cristiano Castelfranchi (2018), "withdrawal is among the action tendencies it elicits" (pp. 715). Simply stated, shame can cause one to cover up behaviors rather than confront them and be revealed as less than one's ideal self.

Feelings ranging from anger and repudiation to conviction and shame may produce inner turmoil. Organizational behavior scholars Russell S. Cropanzano, Sebastiano Massaro, and William J. Becker (2017), in examining the workings of the deontic justice theory, state, "According to [that theory], . . . individuals often feel principled moral obligations to uphold norms of justice" (p. 733) and the "moral treatment of others" (p. 734). It follows that when you awake to the reality that you have been in part responsible for upholding a system that is historically imbalanced in the treatment of certain groups, you may be conflicted. An example of positive deontic justice is, in some cases, the reparations given to Indigenous nations because of the injurious dealings of the early North American colonial settlers. An example of negative deontic justice would be the popular *manifest destiny* thinking that gave Europeans the "God-given right" to take over the land from non-Christians in North America, regardless of the consequences for those people.

To assuage unpleasant emotions, it's easiest to simply turn away; guilt is not necessarily a precursor to action. But for educators who desire to make a difference in the lives of their students, it's imperative to use these reflections to move beyond unpleasant emotions. While guilt may not be a predictor of action, researchers Fabrice Teroni and Otto Bruun (2011) point out that there are "ties between guilt and morality." If you are feeling unease, let it be a motivator. Guilt can be good, as writer Libby Copeland (2018) tells us: "Guilt, by prompting us to think more deeply about our goodness, can encourage humans to atone for errors and fix relationships. Guilt, in other words, can help hold a cooperative species together. It is a kind of social glue."

Take the information you are gathering in your reflections and use it to create a plan of action. The first step is to find an accountability partner or group.

Find an Accountability Partner

Finding at least one other person who is also working toward creating more inclusive campuses and classrooms will give you someone to talk through your emotions and create an accountability cohort with. Who in your environment can you reach out to? Who can you motivate, and who can motivate you? If you are in a diverse environment, this may be an easy task. However, simply finding a coworker who is Black, Asian American and Pacific Islander (AAPI), LGBTQ+, or another marginalized group and asking for a personal diversity guru is inadvisable. It's a little like trying to get the kid in the first row to do your homework for you when you don't talk to that kid otherwise. Further, it singles out people who are already a part of a marginalized group and burdens them further with the task of educating you and being the voice of that entire cultural group.

Your journey should be led by your own quest for knowledge and desire to support others. Be on the lookout for colleagues who:

- Notice and course-correct inequities in curriculum content
- Devote campus and classroom spaces to diverse stories and holidays
- Encourage and push students from nondominant groups even when test scores paint a negative picture
- Develop strong relationships with diverse groups of students

You may already know other educators who are looking to be more culturally responsive, but if you don't, particularly if you are in a low-diversity or politically conservative environment, you may just have to follow the breadcrumbs. In addition to the cues in the previous list, look for diverse classroom libraries, silence in the face of negative comments around race or identity, and that teacher whose doorway is always crowded with diverse sets of students.

If you can't find a coterie of like-minded people in your immediate surroundings, consider joining a book study or fitness class with people who don't look like you, or make connections with like-minded educators on social media. Table 2.1 includes some of the people and hashtags I follow on Twitter, Instagram, and TikTok. See who they follow and find your own favorites. Social media posts can be personal. All these accounts might not speak to you, but for sure you will find among them something to suit your tastes.

Table 2.1: Social Media Accounts for Help Finding an Accountability Partner or Group

Topic	Twitter	Instagram	TikTok
History and first-person information on Indigenous American, AAPI, Latinx, LGBTQ+, Arabic, and Black communities	@LGBTHM @AAPIWomenLead @hispanictips	@antiracismcalendar @lgbt_history	#Nativetiktok @arabicmclovin
Authors, educators, organizations, and hashtags providing information and resources to support teaching diverse populations	@DrIbram (Ibram X. Kendi) #SmallBites @WorldProfessor (Walter D. Greason)	@indigenouseducators @bree.newsome (Bree Newsome Bass) @learnforjustice (Learning for Justice)	@adamlevineperes (also on YouTube) #HispanicHistory #BlackHistory

When You're Ready for Change but Others Are Not

Perhaps you are not feeling uncomfortable; perhaps you simply recognize that your homogenous background didn't provide you with an opportunity to have experience with racial inequities. Now that you have come to a new place of understanding, perhaps you are energized and *ready* to make changes. You may have found that reflecting on your biases and ways of othering has prepared you to rethink your stance on social justice issues, and you may have a clear vision of what your team, campus, or district needs to change to revolutionize the way you educate all students. However, while some may share your enthusiasm for change, *we've always done it this way* is a powerful anchor and not everyone will be as enthusiastic about change as you are. Although you see a need for change, colleagues, school leaders, parents, and even your own family and friends may have difficulties with the new social justice advocate in you.

The values, perceptions, and knowledge you acquire over time are your truths. In your newfound knowledge, you see an opportunity to institute change that will positively impact your learning community. For others, however, your desire for change may represent a personal identity challenge. The administrator in your low-diversity district may not feel that such sweeping change is necessary for the few students outside your school's main demographic. The teacher next door may feel that cultural sensitivity shifts and even professional development are just liberal propaganda.

To avoid conflict, realize that you, as well as they, are all on a journey. Just as you differentiate for students who learn in different ways, you may have to adapt your message to your audience in order to reach your goals for more inclusive classrooms and campuses. Consider decorating a multicultural bulletin board or donating one diverse book to your grade level's class libraries. One recast bulletin board or one new book may not seem like a lot, but a series of small changes makes a big impact over time. Also, try humanizing the items on your call-to-action list. For instance, instead of a vague item about pronouns, highlight the need to support Michael's and Chet's choices of pronouns and names to allow educators to unify around support of current students. When garnering support, try making your conversations about specific changes that impact specific students in your student body rather than systemic overhauls.

When communicating with others about bias in a way that may cause them to feel guilt or discomfort, how you use your words makes a big difference. For instance, instead of calling people out, you can call them in. *Calling in* means to exchange, rather than present, ideas. Calling in means you model best practice and refrain, whenever possible, from giving unsolicited advice. Calling in means that listeners feel heard and respected, whether or not they share your beliefs. It means that you value working with them toward better outcomes.

Some examples of calling in include the following statements.

- "Wow, you do amazing boards for holidays. I want to add boards for Ramadan, Hanukkah, and Chinese New Year on my wall. Will you help me?"

- "I notice James is out in the hall a lot when he has your class. I know he really likes race cars; how about I bring my husband's album on race car specs? Maybe he can come into my room and use the stats from the book to do some of the equations you're learning about?"

- "I'm sure you didn't mean it to be, but I found what you said belittling. Can you give me some clarification on what you really meant?"

Whenever possible, private conversations that assume good intent are generally best practice with sensitive topics. However, sometimes a pattern of behavior emerges, and a stronger stance might be necessary. Make sure that your stronger stance is:

- Act based

- Civil and unemotional

- Centered on student outcomes and campus culture

Using the preceding example, a stronger stance might be, "I see that you put James out in the hall during your class on a regular basis for disciplinary reasons, and I notice he is currently failing your class. Missing instructional time is not in his best interest. I'm willing to help find a solution if you like; if not, let's talk with the team lead to see how we can get him on track."

In contrast to the more conciliatory practice of calling in, *calling out* is reserved for when colleagues show a pattern of undervaluing students, parents, or peers; display a fixed mindset about student growth, especially about growth in students from certain populations; and regularly reject efforts to incorporate more diverse learning materials and culturally responsive pedagogies.

You should call out exceedingly sparingly, after all other attempts at coming together have failed. The motivation for calling out should never be to show how evolved you are; in fact, when calling out, the focus should not be on you or the person being called out. The focus should be on specific behaviors and irrefutable facts backed by data. When calling peers out, be prepared for conflict. Some questions to consider before calling out a peer include the following.

- Will you be able to stand your ground even if retaliatory acts ensue?

- Will you risk job security or be seen as a troublemaker?

- Will your coworker be able to take in what you say, or is the problem bigger than what can effectively be handled at the peer level?

Teachers are often taken to task by parents, peers, and districts for calling out or taking a strong stand, so make sure that when you take a stand, you have a community around you and that you are ready for some pushback. Figure 2.3 (page 28) provides a few examples of calling out versus calling in.

Educators you address may already feel that their interactions with certain populations need to have better outcomes. They may even already feel some sense of guilt, which may cause them to react unfavorably to your calling in or out. It's important to approach any uncomfortable conversations with as much grace and magnanimity as possible. Managing any feelings of guilt that might hinder constructive action and helping others to get comfortable with being uncomfortable moves you one step closer to creating a more diverse and inclusive campus environment. To further explore the differences between calling in and calling out, review the situations in figure 2.4 (page 30) and write down examples of different responses. Doing so will allow you to practice coming up with appropriate responses if you possibly find yourself in an uncomfortable situation with peers.

Calling-Out Nonexample	Calling-Out Example	Calling-In Example	Comparison	Possible Pushback
"You refuse to change with the times." "You need to celebrate all holidays." "Even people who celebrate Christmas aren't into the religious part of the holiday."	"According to current research, that is no longer best practice." "We need to include all holidays." "It's every teacher's duty to support everyone's beliefs."	"Your bulletin boards are amazing, but we have 7 percent Jewish students and 19 percent Muslim students, as well as 12 percent who don't celebrate Christmas. Since our district has a policy of supporting all the cultures and religions represented in our community, let's work together to adhere to the policy."	Calling out poorly is antagonistic and judgmental. This tactic is likely to put a colleague on the defensive. Calling out by directly addressing an issue is sometimes necessary after softer methods have failed.	Even with calling in, a teacher may not want to be corrected or may simply not share your views. Your best options are to model exemplar work and find someone who shares your opinion to work with.
"You do know kicking someone out of class is wrong, right?" "You should sign up for the social-emotional learning and diversity trainings."	"Exclusionary discipline is no longer best practice." "Since exclusionary discipline is no longer best practice, what other suggestions do you have?"	"James was outside your classroom twelve times this month. I noted the days in my calendar because I am concerned that he is missing so much mathematics instruction. How can I help?"	You statements are never a way to garner support for your position. An I, we, or neutral statement is always the better choice. Being solution oriented also makes the conversation about solving a problem rather than keeping the focus on the team member's choices.	You may be met with responses like, "Why are you watching my classroom?" and such a response is valid. Keep focus on the data and keep your concern centered on the student, rather than the teacher. Consider offering to host James in your class to complete his mathematics assignments if that's feasible.

| "Your Black students always complain about you, which is probably why they aren't learning in your class. They think you're racist." | "According to school data, your Black students perform consistently lower in your classes than they do in other classes." | "Saying Black students will never get any smarter negatively impacts your ability to teach your Black students. In our last three data dives, I noticed your Black students performed 6 percentage points lower than our school average for that demographic. What kinds of changes do you need to make to ensure that all our students are getting the education they deserve?" | Citing a complaint based on student gossip is unprofessional. Using data to address an issue is helpful, but be mindful that the teacher's bias may not be the only impacting factor. | Again, focus on the data. No one wants to be called out, in particular when there is data. However, this is the best way to keep the complaint focused on student needs. Be aware, though, that these kinds of interactions may put you on the outs with your colleagues. Change is hard, especially if the need for change is not equally apparent to all stakeholders. |

Figure 2.3: Examples of calling out versus calling in.

Scenario	Calling-In Response	Calling-Out Response
A teacher keeps calling a student named Jesús (pronounced *Hay-soos*) "Geezuz."		
A teacher regularly comments that "those students" can't do gifted and talented or Advanced Placement work.		
A sixth-grade teacher persists in addressing a transgender student by the name and pronouns listed in student records, even after being repeatedly reminded to use a different name and the pronouns *they/them*.		
A teacher regularly compliments but also touches a student's hair.		

Figure 2.4: Calling-in responses versus calling-out responses.

*Visit **go.SolutionTree.com/diversityandequity** for a free reproducible version of this figure.*

When reading your practice answers from figure 2.4, look for a clear difference between the calling-in and calling-out solutions. Calling in approaches the situation in a nonconfrontational way that assumes best intent. Calling out is a direct reproach that addresses an intentional pattern and should be used as a last resort. It should always be student centered, based in irrefutable fact, and supported by data whenever possible.

Reflection to Action

Now it's time to take out your journal again. Hopefully, it's not far away. Again, go through the following questions and answer them thoughtfully. Use this time to deepen your reflection and make note of anything that especially caught your attention. Finally, make yourself a call to action based on what you learned in this chapter. Remember, no goal is too small. You can eat the elephant one small bite at a time.

1. Have you identified any areas of guilt that possibly affect your practice? What are they?

2. How will you push beyond your biases to give students equitable learning opportunities?

3. Who can you enlist as an accountability partner? What qualities do you think make this person a good partner? What might you learn from this person? What can this person learn from you?

4. What actions can you take, or resources can you share, to help other educators grow in this area without being the bearer of recurring unsolicited advice?

In table 2.2, you will find ways to implement what you have learned in this chapter. If you had difficulties coming up with your own call to action, you will find ideas here.

Table 2.2: Sharing What I've Learned About Trading Guilt for Accountability

Group	Activity
Littles (preK–grade 3)	Using whatever art supplies you prefer, have students pair up and make Venn diagrams comparing and contrasting them and their partners. Have them talk about the ways they are the same and different. Suggest students consider things like eye, hair, or skin color; number of siblings and parents; or favorite ice cream, cereal, and colors. Ask students why differences are important and how they enrich a group. Make a class pledge to be kind and inclusive.
Middles (grades 4–7)	Have students make the same kind of Venn diagram, but extend choices to more complex ones like identity, beliefs, or even hobbies and favorite music genres. Ask students why choices and identities should all be valued equally. Ask students what kinds of situations might not be valued equitably, for example, assuming a household headed by a single mom is a "broken home" versus seeing the nuclear family model as the only example of a whole one. Stress the importance of respecting one another and have them create a poster or digital flyer campaign to be a visual reminder of the respect they learned for the kinds of differences that came up in the discussion. Some examples of differences that they might highlight include the following: for reading, Braille books and standard print books; for sports, Paralympics and Olympics; or for social studies or health, diverse couples and familial models.

continued →

Group	Activity
Secondary	Use the same exercise in two parts. In the first part, group students together by asking them to choose someone with whom they are only remotely acquainted. The second part should have groups research divergent ideological profiles like Christian and Muslim; Republican and Democrat; socialist and capitalist; and so on. Have them examine the similarities between the divergent pairs and discuss why they think there is often such strife between groups. Have students pose solutions and create a "say this, not that" chart to help students respond more respectfully to those with whom they disagree.
Staff	Have staff complete the second high school activity and then discuss how discussing divergent ideologies impacts their teaching and how they relate to team members. Have educators role-play to come up with ways to model civil disagreement as well as ways to ensure respectful, civil disagreements in the classroom.
Parents and Community	Send student exemplars of the Venn diagram exercises home in a newsletter. Offer prizes for students and families who create their own family Venn diagrams to become more mindful of biases and othering in the home. For example, a family of six would have a Venn diagram consisting of six circles with the shared home in the middle. Families could also complete a collection of Venn diagrams with two or three circles each.

CHAPTER THREE

Bias, Labels, and Language

When I was a little girl, James Brown's iconic refrain "Say it loud—I'm Black and I'm proud" (Brown & Ellis, 1968) was as interwoven into the Black community's culture as the words of James Weldon Johnson's (n.d.) "Lift Every Voice and Sing"; I still remember at gatherings as a child singing, "Sing a song full of the faith that the dark past has taught us. Sing a song full of the hope that the present has brought us." For my great-grandmother, however, us calling ourselves Black was shameful and offensive. She could barely even abide being called a Negro because it was too close to "that other word." My great-grandmother was "colored," period. She had grown up in a time when the saying was, "If you're White, you're alright; if you're brown, stick around; if you're Black, get back," a popular paraphrasing of the song "Black, Brown and White" written in the 1930s or 1940s by William Lee Conley "Big Bill" Broonzy (2000) and eventually recorded by him in 1952. She explained to me that we are all different shades and colors of brown—colored—not Black. It made sense when I was little, because I left the faces of people in my coloring book uncolored if they were White and I colored them in if I wanted them brown. As I got older, I remember questioning that logic and thinking that White people were more shades of pink and peach, making them colored too, but I was not going to "back talk."

As the label *Black* became more widely used, I just attributed my great-grandmother's insistence on the use of "colored" to her age, thinking, as many young people do about their elders, that she was old-fashioned and prone to espouse outdated notions.

Now, through the lens of a woman getting closer to a grandmother's age than I care to admit, I've realized that she had experienced the word *Black* being weaponized, and no amount of James Brown's singing and dancing could change that for her.

Many times, people use labels and language, sometimes purposefully, sometimes inadvertently, in ways that disadvantage the people they reference. It may not be easy to keep up with ever-changing identity concepts, designations, and descriptors, but it is critical to be aware of those changes so that you do not cling to outdated and harmful terms and epithets. That's why the third guiding principle is to use bias-free descriptors and language, as shown in figure 3.1.

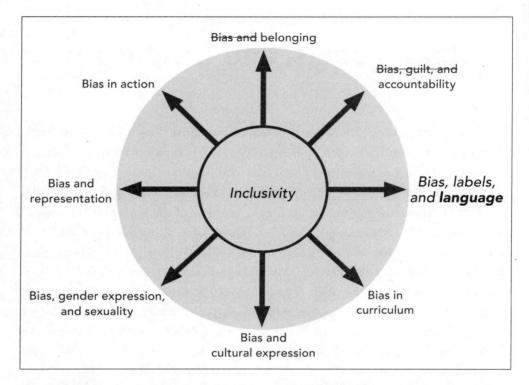

Figure 3.1: Guiding principle 3—Use bias-free descriptors and language.

Bias is often embedded in labels and descriptors. In being unaware of the subtleties of meanings, educators can unintentionally show racialism, ableism, sexism, classism, and so on during staff, student, and parent interactions. Sometimes, it's not the spoken word but actions that speak for us, communicating bias just as loudly. This chapter explores the ways language and action can signal bias and helps educators make more inclusive choices.

Bias-Free Language

Language is always evolving and changing. As Betty Birner (n.d.), editor for the Linguistic Society of America, points out, "New technologies, new products, and new experiences require new words to refer to them clearly and efficiently." For example, a premillennial world could not have foreseen *google* (that is, to use a search engine to obtain information about someone or something on the internet) becoming a verifiable verb, one that many style guides no longer even capitalize. And I may be dating myself, but I could not imagine that I would be colored, Negro, <u>b</u>lack, African American, and <u>B</u>lack in one lifetime—and who knows what's still to come.

There are many ways in which our language can be biased, inaccurate, or even weaponized. *Blondes*, *suits*, *liberal*, and *conservative*, for example, all carry social connotations beyond their literal definitions. Further, qualifiers like *devout* Christians or *radical* Muslims create an environment in which cultures or religions are either accepted and praised or perceived as threatening. Since the Civil Rights era, the educational community has made some headway and begun to place an emphasis on language descriptors. For example, in the special education community, inclusive educators are conscientious about referring to *students with disabilities* rather than *disabled students*—a person-first choice. If that's new to you, special education scholars and advocates Michelle Foley and Cristina Santamaría Graff (2018) go into depth about student-centered labeling. In figure 3.2, you can practice rewriting the terms listed with as much person-first specificity as possible.

Commonly Used Labels	Person-First Terminology
Example: Special education teacher	Ms. Salinas
Autistic student	
Special education students	
Wheelchair-bound student	
The disabled or handicapped teacher	

Figure 3.2: Practice rewriting terms in person-first language.

*Visit **go.SolutionTree.com/diversityandequity** for a free reproducible version of this figure.*

In figure 3.3 (page 36), review possible answers to the prompts in figure 3.2 and compare them to your own. In addition to terms provided, reflect on whether there is a legitimate need to use a descriptor. If the person's name suffices, choose that instead of a descriptor.

But what about even more subtle linguistic choices? It turns out our language and labels, like *SPED kid* or *Title I kids*, may not only be offensive or stigmatizing but also have more measurable consequences. According to education scientists

Commonly Used Labels	Person-First Terminology
Example: Special education teacher	Ms. Salinas
Autistic student	The seventh grader with autism
Special education students	The students
	The students in room 221
	The students receiving special education services
	Students with IEPs
Wheelchair-bound student	Student who uses a wheelchair
The disabled or handicapped teacher	The teacher
	The teacher who uses or has crutches (or a wheelchair, a prosthesis, and so on)

Figure 3.3: Possible responses to practicing rewriting terms in person-first language.

Samantha G. Daley and Gabrielle Rappolt-Schlichtmann (2018), those stigmas can make significant differences in academic performance, "particularly in academic situations that are likely to be threatening due to stereotypes." Further, antideficit researchers Krystal L. Williams, Justin A. Coles, and Patrick Reynolds (2020) add, "Dominant narratives [that equate Black students with poor academic performance] have negatively affected Black students' experiences and . . . overarching academic trajectories" (p. 249). Your word choices and even your tone make a difference in what your students believe about themselves, so choosing what you say and how you say it are central to countering stereotypes and everything that comes with them. Let's say you have a student from the special education department with dyslexia who lacks confidence because he reads far below grade level. Let's say the same student is extremely gifted in mathematics but can only do word problems if they are read aloud. You could exclaim, "Wow, you're really good at this!" showing him how little you were expecting of him, or you could tell him that he has a real future in mathematics and have him pair with a good reader who struggles with mathematics. The latter choice would develop not only his mathematics aptitude but his confidence as well.

When considering race and identity, it's understandably hard to know what terms are currently "politically correct." In 2020 alone, I was labeled black, Black, African American, person of color, woman of color, she/her, and BIPOC (Black, Indigenous, and people of color). And those are only skin-deep labels. While you may not always be able to approach language and labels confidently in an ever-evolving society, your students depend on you doing your best to send messaging that is race, gender, and ability affirming.

When it comes to language bias, the American Psychological Association (APA) Style (2019) guide's online page on bias-free language (https://bit.ly/3lT3Vjy) is the consummate resource for up-to-date information on gender-, race-, and ability-neutral terms. There you will find general guidelines as well as research background, specific terminology, and detailed usage recommendations. Figure 3.4 includes some useful bias-free linguistic updates that may be helpful to teachers and students in the 21st century classroom.

Say This	Not This
Chair, mail carrier, firefighter, flight attendant, nurse, congressional representative, human beings	Chairman, mailman, fireman, stewardess, male nurse, congressman, mankind
Student in a wheelchair, student with a learning disability, students who are neurodiverse	Handicapped student, learning disability student, special education students
African American, Black, BIPOC	Negro, colored, black, Afro-American
Pakistani, Nigerian, Vietnamese	Indian or Asian, African, Asian
Mexican American, Cuban American, Latinx, Korean, Nigerian, Chinese American, Congolese American	Hispanics (when the culture is known), Latino or Latina (unless the gender is known), Asians, Africans
Native American or specific tribe name, Indigenous peoples of North America, Inuit, Pacific Islander, AIAN (American Indian and Alaskan Native), API (Asian and Pacific Islander), the term someone self-identifies as (just ask them!)	Indian, Eskimo, Hawaiian, Chinese
Singular they, another sex, of a different sex	He or she, opposite sex

Source: APA Style, 2019.

Figure 3.4: Able-, gender-, and race-neutral terminology examples.

No one term can fully encapsulate and describe a human being. A Nigerian American in your class may simply self-identify as Black. A Mexican student may identify as Latino, Latina, Latinx, Hispanic and White, or just White. A student listed as male may self-identify as female, with no references to her, or *their*, sexuality. Even more important than knowing the most up-to-date, politically correct terms is knowing your students and making them feel included and accepted. Two handy rules are to (1) use the most specific identifier (for example, Chinese instead of Asian or Kenyan instead of African) and (2) ask whenever in doubt.

Another way people use language to convey an exclusive hierarchy of norms that Western civilization is built on is to use an article or demonstrative pronoun in front of a label, as in "the Mexicans," "the gays," "those Muslims," "those people," and so on. Such phrasing reduces people to a homogenous lineup expected to all have the same characteristics and values.

Sometimes, bias is unintentional and comes from personal curiosity or even the desire to build cultural competence. As researchers Tina M. Harris, Anastacia Janovec, Steven Murray, Sneha Gubbala, and Aspen Robinson (2019) find, many innocent attempts at gleaning knowledge are "actual manifestations of aversive racism" (p. 72). Further, microaggression trauma experts Kevin L. Nadal, Tanya Erazo, and Rukiya King (2019) tell us the language we use can not only hinder academic performance but also cause trauma. This kind of trauma, while invisible to the naked eye, affects students in long-lasting ways, much in the way that post-traumatic stress disorder affects veterans.

Figure 3.5 lists examples of questions that can unintentionally cause trauma, with context as to why they are inappropriate in most situations.

Questions like these not only miss the mark when creating inclusive spaces but also work to create or maintain an *us* versus *them* environment. These small but significant slights are called microaggressions, and we will explore them more in depth in chapter 8 (page 113). Students from underrepresented communities experience this feeling of not belonging on a daily basis. Nadal and his colleagues (2019) tell us that throughout the 2010s, hundreds of academic papers and thousands of media articles have documented subtle linguistic and even nonverbal forms of racism, which we will discuss later in this chapter.

Not only questions, but statements, assumptions, and racially motivated assertions given as compliments can further harm attempts to create inclusive classrooms and campuses. Figure 3.6 presents some examples of statements and why they are manifestations of racism or bias.

Policy Language

Words in curricula and policies can often target individuals who don't belong to the dominant culture. I remember the first time I wore a braided hairstyle to work. My supervisor called me in to her office to ask me how long my hair would "be like that." This was at a time when hair policies were constrained to "neat and well

Questions	Why the Question Is a Manifestation of Racism or Bias
"Can you get a sunburn?"	The question assumes that melanin provides mythical protection from the ills of humanity and wards off damaging effects of the sun, like skin cancer (it doesn't). This train of thought is akin to the still-prevalent notion that darker-skinned individuals do not feel pain in the same way that lighter-skinned individuals do.
"Did you win a scholarship?"	This question, asked of someone who does not look like the majority of a school's population, particularly at elite, private schools and universities, is an automatic assumption that the student does not belong and does not merit a place at the institution.
"Can I touch your hair?" or "Can I see your hair?"	Uninvited touching about the face and head is a violation of personal space and assumes that the individual is an outsider or a curiosity rather than a peer. If a person's hair is covered, particularly with a hijab, the question demonstrates a lack of cultural knowledge and respect.
"Where are you *really* from?"	This question assumes, often incorrectly, that a student is not a native and does not belong. It also assumes that everyone from a country looks like people from the dominant culture in a country.

Figure 3.5: Questions that stem from biased or racist notions.

Statements	Why the Statement Is a Manifestation of Racism or Bias
"I didn't know [cultural or ethnic group] [verb and activity]." (For example, "I didn't know Asians played basketball.")	The assumption is that culture is monolithic so that certain groups don't engage in certain activities, listen to certain kinds of music, or visit certain places.
"You're so articulate."	This assumes that being articulate is not the norm for certain groups.
"You're really pretty for a [cultural or ethnic group]."	Qualifying any compliment rescinds the compliment, and being "pretty, but . . ." usually implies some lack as measured against the "norm."
"But you don't [act, look, or sound] [cultural or ethnic group]." (For example, "But you don't sound Black.")	The assumption here is that the receiver of the "compliment" is more like the giver of the compliment and is therefore better than others who share a similar cultural identity with the receiver.

Figure 3.6: Statements that stem from biased or racist notions.

groomed," leaving styles that did not mimic Eurocentric hairstyles in the "not neat and not well-groomed" category. She never used the words inappropriate or unprofessional, but her messaging was clear.

California's Create a Respectful and Open Workplace for Natural Hair (CROWN) Act (2019), effective January 1, 2020, is the first law banning discrimination based on hairstyles. This is significant in the wake of several lawsuits against school districts, such as those discussed in attorney D. Sharmin Arefin's (2020) American Bar Association article, "Is Hair Discrimination Race Discrimination?" These lawsuits are becoming more commonplace because of policies that discriminate against natural hairstyles. A *natural hairstyle* is a style designed for textured hair that does not require chemical or heat-based straightening to emulate the styles easily attained by people with straight hair. Schools have also come under fire in the media for banning styles like afros and locs, both natural hairstyles.

One 2018 incident captures the essence and extent of natural hair discrimination. A referee, citing state interscholastic athletics rules, refused to let a Buena, New Jersey, high school wrestler compete unless he cut his locs (Osborne, 2018). Locs, also known as dreadlocks, take years to grow, and when they are cut, they can unravel, which necessitates cutting the hair down to a short afro. At the wrestling meet, the referee forced the teen to choose between forfeiting his match and letting down his team or submitting to a public haircut in a gym full of onlookers. Luckily, this caused backlash, and the referee was disciplined, though unfortunately not in time to stop the incident in real time. This indicates a much bigger issue. Reporter Laurel Wamsley's (2018) article took a statement from Rajhon White, a Buena alum, who said, "The fact that the adults in the gym let that haircut happen reflects a larger problem with the culture of the community." The message here is the self-esteem-damaging implication that hair in its natural state is neither professional nor well groomed or is not considered acceptable when measured by the "ideal" standard.

Other non-inclusive words are found in *look policies* for dance or cheer squads. These are policies that exclude applicants based on weight, height, body type, and sometimes skin color, rather than ability. Schools develop these policies through a Eurocentric lens that uses White ideals of beauty as normative. As psychology scholar Huberta Jackson-Lowman (2014) recounts in her publication "An Analysis of the Impact of Eurocentric Concepts of Beauty on the Lives of Afrikan American Women," "Throughout the world the globalization of Eurocentric standards of beauty has resulted in the development of industries that support it, the marketing of images that reify it, the structuring of policies that reward it, and the enactment of interpersonal and personal behavioral routines that emulate it." In short, even when there is no official written policy, students who don't fit the "norm" acutely feel silent disparaging.

Assessment Language

The language educators use in testing can also be at odds with creating a sense of belonging. While worlds beyond the literacy voting tests of the 1900s, which used discriminatory practices to disenfranchise voters from minority groups, testing still has not advanced enough to be a true measure of knowledge, and that has largely to do with linguistic and cultural biases.

Not only are there many unfamiliar settings and cultural references in standardized testing, the language poses challenges to English learners and others. Venn diagrams, for instance, are common in the United States but unfamiliar in other countries; and when was the last time you heard *all of the above* spoken in any conversational setting? Standardized tests are considered in educational circles to be objective, almost scientific instruments to measure learning outcomes. However, as educational researchers Matthew Knoester and Wayne Au (2017) report, "High-stakes, standardized testing, and the meritocratic assumptions that serve to underpin it, also create another self-reinforcing cycle of racism that serves as a proxy for the expression of whiteness." Assumptions about what should be common knowledge can pose problems for all students, but those assumptions are particularly problematic for students who may not use standard English at home or for those who have limited academic language proficiency.

Some test developers have begun to make changes by offering what they believe to be multicultural settings and wording, which is a start. Seeing Don Julio and Jameka go to the store instead of Dick and Jane may help students see themselves reflected in academic materials, but the syntax and colloquialisms are often still foreign. While language bias in standardized testing is outside educators' locus of control, there are ways to scaffold academic language skill building to better prepare your students and help make sure that they don't feel like outsiders, especially with content they understand well.

The use of translation dictionaries is a common testing accommodation, but scaffolding requires more than the structures that are already in place. Because many English learners have limited academic language proficiency in their native language, they may not understand the meaning of words they look up. According to Colorín Colorado (n.d.), a leading English learner education resource, research shows that students who lack prior instruction or support in academic language development in their native language may take seven years to develop this proficiency, as opposed to the five years it takes other learners.

To help close this gap, teachers should use social English to teach academic English by integrating diverse languages and dialects in classroom discussions. Students can review or retell stories, summarize texts and concepts in songs or poetry, or simply think-pair-share in their native language.

Linguistics scholars Blake Turnbull and Moyra Sweetnam Evans's (2017) study on the reading skills of Japanese English-learner students found that "discussing language 2 texts in the language 1 facilitates the accessing of higher-level language 1 reading skills by language 2 readers" (p. 147). Simply stated, students holding discussions in their native language (language 1) on texts read in a second language (language 2) comprehend more. By building a bridge between native languages and both academic and social language, students will have the chance to build on what they know to critically process academic information. This strategy will help prepare them for standardized tests and has the additional benefit of validating cultural identities.

Making diverse languages and cultural expressions welcome in the classroom gives educators a perfect opportunity to build cultural bridges. One day, for example, after reprimanding a student, a student asked me if I was going to give him the *chancla*, which brought on a fit of laughter from the class. In Hispanic communities, *la chancla* (Spanish for slipper, or flip-flop) is a legendary term, signaling that a spanking is coming. This sparked a conversation in our very diverse class about how mamas all over the world say some version of "*Te voy a dar con la chancla*!" ("I'm going to give you the *chancla*!"). As it turns out, the wording may vary, but the concept of a catchphrase indicating big, you've-crossed-the-line trouble is a part of mom culture all over the world.

In my own anecdotal research, I recounted the funny story to all my classes throughout the day. And it turned out that several cultures, including mainstream U.S. ones, have variations of *la chancla*. The question is, Would students know the English word for *la chancla*, which is usually translated as *slipper*? *House shoes*, maybe; *slides* or *flip-flops*, probably. But *slipper*? An online search of Texas's standardized test, STAAR, and the term *slipper* yields pages of results indicating the use of the word *slipper* on tests. Considering that fable and fairy tale culture centered around Aesop and the Grimm brothers is fast giving way to more modern and culturally diverse offerings, *slipper* may not come to mind unless a student is familiar with Cinderella. As a matter of fact, as I recounted the story throughout the day, the word *slipper* never came up. This is just one example of a word on standardized tests that holds no meaning for many of our students. Still, the tests aren't going away any time soon, so teaching obscure testing vocabulary is key.

Here are a few ways to build bridges between native languages and English.

- Ask students to repeat a certain phrase in their first language.

- Encourage multilingual *turn and talks*. When analyzing texts and discussing concepts, students can talk to each other in a shared language or explain concepts in both languages in order to compare and contrast subtle differences.

- Use an online search function such as Google Translate (https://translate .google.com) or DeepL Translator (www.deepl.com) to find words and learn to pronounce them in other languages.

- Introduce a vocabulary or concept word in more than one language. Have students look up definitions in more than one language.

- Pepper lessons with big idea words or phrases in the languages of your English learners. If the lesson is on the butterfly life cycle, for example, find and use life cycle words in the languages your students speak. Alternately, find and use the words in Spanish even to enrich a classroom environment in which there are no English learners.

- Use a popular colloquial or slang term to describe an academic concept. If you don't know much slang, ask your students to explain things in "cooler" terms.

- Encourage students to translate vocabulary and concepts as time permits, and always have them learn the academic definition and a definition they write in their own words.

- Assign students to research how to say a phrase in the language of their grandparents or great-grandparents. If necessary, add a few more *greats* to find a second language. If another language is unknown, have students use a language of their choosing.

Everyone is from somewhere originally, so finding out how to say *summarize* or *greater than* in Gaelic, Italian, Spanish, Mandarin, Swahili, or Arabic is an easy way to expand everyone's knowledge of academic concepts and ensure deeper understanding, especially for your English learners. A thirty-second online search will get you what you need. If you can't mimic the pronunciation exactly, don't worry. By learning phrases in new languages, you show that you too are a learner. In placing value on diverse languages, you show not only that you value different cultures but that it's OK not to know words as long as you're willing to learn them. Accepting and incorporating diverse languages is one way to dispel biases and build your own cultural literacy. These lessons will bring you closer to your students and help foster a respectful dynamic, which has many benefits: "Respect can reduce ingroup favoritism and improve intergroup relations" (Eschert & Simon, 2019).

Finally, for your students who are practicing academic discourse, these activities will make assessment language more familiar and help positively impact academic outcomes. Alternately, disallowing diverse languages is an action grounded in bias, often stemming from the regressive notion that in the United States, for example, there is no room for languages other than English. Although you may never utter the words *speak English* to a student, that exclusionary bias can be an action that speaks louder than words.

Actions Speak Louder Than Words

Silent annoyance and unspoken rules damage school culture and student self-esteem as much as outright racism does. Although educators may laud students and celebrate culture on billboards and in culture month celebrations, what we *don't* say is as important or even more important than what we do say. For example, in an environment where teachers allow boys to give an answer out of turn while not calling on girls because they quietly raise their hands before giving an answer, girls get less attention. As a matter of fact, according to the American Association of University Women (n.d.) website, educators tend to expect boys to excel in STEM subjects and even give them a "boys will be boys" pass on violence and misbehavior, while they expect girls to be polite and compliant and steer them away from STEM subjects as early as elementary school.

Often these silent expectations, or at least minimizations, come through content. The absence across content areas of important players who are not White and male leaves the unmistakable impression that only White males are inventors, mathematicians, scientists, and composers. Further, the time that a curriculum spends on what's important in Western classical education and the emphasis it places on Eurocentric standards send the distinct message that Eurocentric and White cultures are valued above all others. Additionally, celebrating diversity only in certain months speaks volumes about the predetermined significance of a group's contributions, and, although well intended, it again raises questions about what educators consider standard ("history") versus nonstandard (*Black* history, *Hispanic* history, *Native American* history, and so on).

It is important to recognize that this damaging language appears in what we say, what we don't say, and even how we group concepts. For example, being aware of pronoun use (such as defaulting to *he* when referring to scientists, programmers, and doctors or *she* when talking about nurses and teachers) makes a difference in whether girls consider STEM careers, according to correlations drawn from cognitive scientists Molly Lewis and Gary Lupyan's (2020) research on male career associations.

Even the way educators assign class jobs can have an effect on role associations. When they assign girls to clean, organize, and walk classmates to the nurse, while asking boys to make the trash run and be physical education team captains, educators are subtly but unmistakably saying that females belong in the home while males should go out and seek adventure. Educators may leave out references to nonbinary students altogether. This is not an intentional slight, just one that builds on common gender roles in larger society. Males taking out the trash is typical in the media and in many homes. UNICEF researcher Nikola Balvin (2017) suggests that gender socialization—like when parents give children different toys to play with (for example, cars for boys, dolls for girls)—affects gender equality and even economics later in life. Figure 3.7 (page 46) provides a snapshot of the far-reaching implications of gender socialization.

To counter bias in classroom socialization, ask yourself if you regularly cast students in archetypical heteronormative gender roles, such as giving boys the balls and sending girls to the dress-up corner. If so, encourage all of your students to play different parts within the social strata of your class. You may find that the person who likes to organize the books or has the neatest handwriting may not be who you've pictured. Further, remember that, according to Gallup, almost one in twenty people self-identifies as a part of the LGBTQ+ community (Newport, 2018). That means in a class of twenty, at least one of your students will fall outside of cishet normative expectations for gender roles or sexuality. Creating an affirming environment means providing diverse books and curriculum materials that reflect all kinds of identities, but mostly it means ensuring that your classroom is a place where each student feels accepted by you and by the other students, who will usually follow your lead.

With the exception of the able-bodied, heterosexual White (Western European descendant) community, since the early 1900s, every community in the United States has had an identity evolution. Although the United States is a country of immigrants, calling a White student a German American or Irish American is not the norm. That unspoken norm establishes White as standard, making everything else substandard. It is foundational to every system in the United States and many other countries, and the subtlety with which it is interwoven is difficult to see if you are White. It is difficult to see beyond if you aren't.

If you have been raised in a more conservative setting, you may have difficulties understanding and relating to the evolving concepts surrounding identity, and that is understandable. In particular, if you are conservative and from a community that has little or no diversity, this chapter may be foreign indeed. Still, with the U.S. Census Bureau (2018) forecasting that White majority culture will become the minority

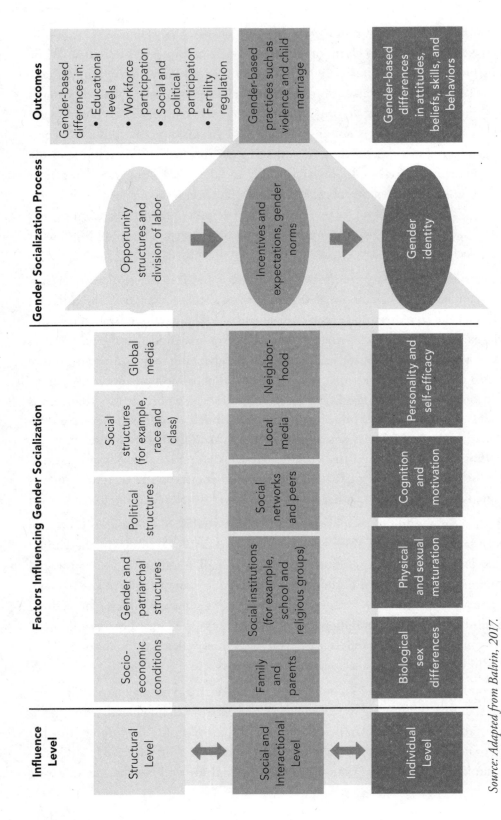

Source: Adapted from Balvin, 2017.

Figure 3.7: Influences impacting gender socialization.

culture by 2045, every educator needs to lay a strong foundation by building a school culture that is welcoming for everyone. That starts with recognizing that the new norm is that there is no norm. As you consider your linguistic choices, be aware of your vantage point—that is, your lived experiences and the perspective from which you view the world. Inclusivity means that you work to ensure as much as within your power that you can understand the world from varying perspectives, not just your own, so that you can let empathy guide your choices.

Reflection to Action

Once again it's time to take out your journal, which by now should be close by. Remember that no one is looking, so be thoughtful and honest as you answer the questions, reflect on your learning, and prepare to implement what you've learned.

1. What are some things that you heard growing up that would be now considered sexist, racist, or hurtful to groups other than your own?

2. What are your own feelings toward growing diversity and the changes in linguistic mores that are taking place across the globe?

3. How can you stay true to yourself and make every student feel accepted and welcome?

4. What phrases in another language or dialect can you learn and integrate to help students build bridges to academic language?

Use your reflections to make a personal call to action. If your journaling did not reveal any personal calls to action that you're ready to take, in table 3.1 you will find activities on bias in language that you can implement in class or in your community.

Table 3.1: Sharing What I've Learned About Bias-Free Descriptors and Language

Group	Activity
Littles (preK–grade 3)	Read books with diverse human characters and ask students to describe the characters they read about. Give students proper terms and identifiers, using figures 3.2 (page 35) and 3.4 (page 37) as guides. Discuss what students have in common with the characters and how they are different.
Middles (grades 4–7)	Have students talk about name-calling and identity-attacking comments they have heard or read. Talk about the importance of person-first language and language that celebrates and respects cultural, religious, and gender identities.

continued →

Group	Activity
Secondary	Extend the previous activity by pulling examples from media and social media. Add to the discussion by reviewing *digital citizenship rules*, which are guidelines that govern online safety and well-being.
Staff	Using figures 3.2 (page 35) and 3.4 (page 37), assign teams the task of googling images of diverse groups of people. Teams should take turns identifying the images. Discuss how bias, both good and bad, plays a role in how people identify images. Accept any insecurity and awkwardness as a part of the learning process. For example, a Somali group might be identified as Black or Arabic; only the team who chose the image will know for sure. Other team members are allowed, even encouraged, to choose wrongly. Creating a safe space to feel uncomfortable, get it wrong, and even apologize to anyone affected and accept forgiveness gives educators practice in navigating uncomfortable conversations and scenarios.
Parents and Community	Use the information in this chapter to create a small multicultural did-you-know section in your newsletter. For example, *Did you know that Onesimus, an enslaved man in Boston, was instrumental in mitigating smallpox by introducing the concept of inoculation to the colonies? Or, Did you know that many cultures all over the world have some type of flatbread? Ethiopian injera, Mexican tortillas, French crepes, American pancakes, and Indian naan are all types of flatbread.* Don't have a newsletter? Have students create one that keeps parents in the know and educates them as well.

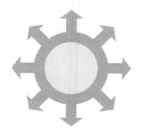

CHAPTER FOUR

Bias in Curriculum

While riding home from school one day when I was a young girl, our car stopped next to a truck at the traffic light. The truck was standard issue for the area—big mud terrain tires, a gun rack, and a red flag with white stars and crossed blue bars in the window. I said to my mom that I wanted one of those flags for my room. She and a friend from work who was also in the car laughed. I pressed on, insisting that the flag was cool and would match my Americana theme. They froze, exchanging a look of incredulity. They asked me one question: "Do you know what that is?"

At that moment, I realized that the stars and bars were indeed not a symbol of Americana or even an alternative, redesigned U.S. flag from the past but in actuality the Confederate flag. I was a junior in high school. That day, after a decade of public education that included both American and Texas history, that one question finally opened my eyes. In that moment, I realized that if the South did indeed rise again, I would likely be expected to don a head wrap and go back to picking cotton on a plantation for my enslaver.

I had managed to live my whole life as a Black person in this alternate reality in which the South and the Confederacy were one glorious part of my past and heritage as a Southerner, never realizing that the heritage for me was not one of glory or an unfair wrenching away of wealth and lifestyle by "those cursed Yankees." On that day, the ground shifted, and I realized that the heroic, brave soldiers of the South were not fighting for me. In all the years that I was taught about the nobility and preeminence of the South, my own heritage was one of enslavement, forced labor, hunger, rape, and other atrocities that were barely touched on in my history classes. As a matter of fact, in the 2015 edition of McGraw-Hill's ninth-grade world geography textbook (Schlanger, 2015), Texas students are still taught about "patterns of immigration" and the "millions of *workers*" (emphasis mine) brought to America from Africa.

This kind of historical rewrite is called erasure. *Erasure* is an intentional or unintentional omission or whitewashing of historical events that excises the contributions of certain populations:

> [This] injustice doesn't only wrong those whose contributions
> to the collective body of knowledge are discounted, excluded,
> or otherwise discredited. It also wrongs those who draw on this
> body of knowledge and those to whom it will be passed down.
> (Mitchell-Yellin, 2019)

In the case of McGraw-Hill's historical rewrite, erasure made the atrocities of grand-scale human trafficking and child labor in the United States easier to read about, but it also neglected to show heroic survival in the face of those atrocities and erased contributions of a whole segment of Americans. Our reluctance to embrace all of our story continues to cause an imbalance in our society; and the curriculum is a big part of that. The fourth guiding principle, represent diverse perspectives through content and curriculum, offers support for educators seeking to counteract erasure by providing diverse instructional materials and exploring diverse historical perspectives (see figure 4.1).

This chapter focuses on the need for multiperspectivity in teaching. This is not only an important concept for history and civics teachers. Across content areas, including fine arts, STEM, and English language arts, educators have a duty to teach civic responsibility through empathy and respect for diverse perspectives. Educators also are the gatekeepers of information, connecting students to the world around them through a rich and transparent rendering of facts, both past and present.

Multiperspectivity

After the brutal death of George Floyd in spring 2020 at the hands of police officers and the ensuing protests, schools, organizations, municipalities, and individuals around the globe began to consider that racism still plays a critical part in our society. Other organizations have, unfortunately, continued to vehemently deny any possibility of systemic racism being the reality for many non-White people around the world. The chasm between these two fronts leaves many educators ill at ease as to what belongs in the classroom and what is better left to the influence of the political and religious ideology of parents. That's where *multiperspectivity* comes in. The word, which has gained traction since the 1990s, describes the opportunity

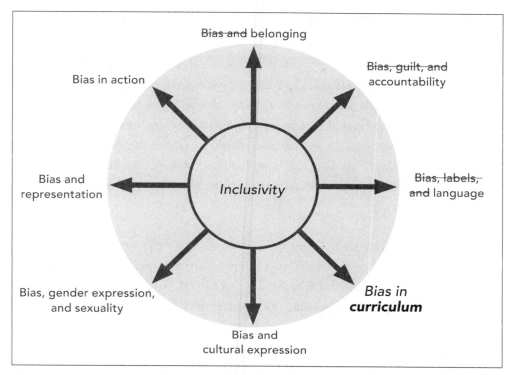

Figure 4.1: Guiding principle 4—Represent diverse perspectives through content and curriculum.

of learning about the past from varied perspectives. For example, to continue my earlier anecdote, I learned all about the glory of the South and the heroic deeds of the Confederate Army. I learned about the proud Texas tradition of flying the Confederate flag, and only as a sidebar did I hear that in owning the pride and glory of the Confederacy, I took a stance in favor of enslavement as a necessary evil—a stance against my own freedom. In reality, the Confederate Army fought against the United States in an act of rebellion. Education that lacked multiperspectivity obscured that point, as it did the horrific idea that the South fought to maintain a social order based on the inhumanity of human trafficking and child labor. A transparent representation would have included stories of soldiers, women, children, the gentry, diverse immigrants, enslaved people, Indigenous peoples, and so on. All of these perspectives together would give us a true picture of those times, much like we get to view a football play from different angles to see the full picture.

The fact is, the United States was built on the founding principles of liberty and justice for all, but our conflicted history with Indigenous peoples and enslaved Africans has yet to live up to those principles. By teaching about the past from various perspectives, educators can acknowledge the greatness of the United States but also the pain it has inflicted on its citizens in that quest for that greatness. Teaching about one without teaching about the other is like letting a father describe how easy the birth was without acknowledging the mother's labor.

Although this section has focused on history, multiperspectivity should not be limited to civics instruction. Mathematics students should know that the father of algebra is Muslim; artists should know that Frida Kahlo was a member of the LGBTQ+ community; English language arts teachers should know the contributions of Korean American writer Mary Paik Lee and Canadian Cree writer Rosanna Deerchild; and musicians should know that classical music is only one important genre of many.

Civics

Courses like history and geography are windows to the world and should be used as such. No matter what your population is, diversity promotes empathy that, according to sociology scholar Elizabeth Segal (2011), finally moves us to build a "framework" to "address disparities." Emphasizing the rich history of great precolonial societies like those in North and West Africa, Asia, and the Americas gives students knowledge that course-corrects the focus of the Western Eurocentric time line that has dominated U.S. perspectives on history.

Although there is some teaching on Mayan, Ancient Chinese, Egyptian, and a few other precolonial societies, educators tend to teach the lion's share of history from the perspective of colonizers, with trade and migration centering on the last five hundred years. In actuality, the world's time line is much longer, and with the internet, there are many more stories to be found and told. Finding and telling those stories will improve teacher-student relationships and student outcomes by reducing stereotype threat, which will in turn make way for better academic outcomes. As researchers Markus Appel and Nicole Kronberger (2012) tell us, "The anxiety stemming from stereotype threat [is] known to result in much lower performance on tests." *Stereotype threat* is the pressure that groups from the nondominant culture feel because of the risk of confirming negative stereotypes about their cultural group. When educators paint positive pictures of diverse populations, students feel a greater sense of belonging, which lessens this anxiety and cements relationships.

First-Person Stories

When teaching history, remember that stories are personal and that perspectives vary. A proud father may talk about the crushing pain as his hand was held too tightly in the labor room. The woman holding his hand would describe crushing pain differently. A woman who desires, but is unable, to experience childbirth would describe pain, once again, differently.

Reflect on what you were taught in school. Ask yourself the following questions.

- Why did explorers "claim" foreign lands for their countries of origin?

- Why are Black history, Hispanic history, Asian American history, and so on not just history?

- How did European immigrants of the 1800s become "White" as opposed to German American, Irish American, Greek American, and so on?

- Who were the bad guys in the wars Indigenous peoples fought to keep their land?

- Why was it considered acceptable to subjugate people who were or are culturally or religiously dissimilar?

- How could the United States be pro "liberty and justice for all" and simultaneously pro enslavement and pro Indian reservations?

When reflecting on these questions, consider that your answers may or may not be the same as the answers from your students. But also consider, more importantly, that history is a subject that should invite your students to ask questions and draw conclusions about the world and people around them.

Bias in curriculum occurs largely because history is constructed from one point of view that excludes other stories from the same time periods. According to the Stanford History Education Group (n.d.), quoting history educator and author Ann Low-Beer, "In history, multiple perspectives are usual and have to be tested against evidence, and accounted for in judgments and conclusions." The big idea is that history is a multiperspective reconstruction rather than a first-person definitive account.

As you seek to educate future generations, consider checking the Smithsonian, the Library of Congress, and the National Park Service for primary documents and stories to round out and give perspective to what you find in textbooks. Here are a few examples.

- The National Park Service's *Telling All Americans' Stories* series (www.nps .gov/subjects/tellingallamericansstories/index.htm)

- The Library of Congress's digital collections with original letters, treaties, maps, and pictures (www.loc.gov/collections/)

- The Smithsonian Online Virtual Archives featuring collections organized by topics and museum (https://sova.si.edu/)

Students can explore the 1800s from the perspective of an Indigenous medicine woman, folk music from a collection of almost five thousand songs, and original family documents from Alexander Graham Bell. Educators shouldn't have to hide certain stories or teach students about mythical perfection so that they can see greatness in the story of the United States. Learning about what the forefathers achieved as humans rather than perfect icons will let students know that perfection does not produce greatness; owning failings and persevering does. Benjamin Franklin is a perfect example. At the beginning of his life, he believed in enslavement, but before his death, he became president of an abolitionist group and freed his own slaves (PBS, 2002). Learning about the many stories and perspectives that make up the tapestry of the United States will help students develop empathy through history.

Untold Stories Matter

State standards call for educating even kindergarten students in family and community life and teaching them about state and national traditions, customs, and historical figures. Finding materials that include diverse families and family models is easy. Reaching out in person or virtually to find community workers who represent diverse cultures should also pose no problem. But finding materials on significant people who shaped the nation who were not White and male is much more difficult. For example, Chief Powhatan (whose proper name was Wahunsenacawh), who began negotiations with the Jamestown settlers in 1607, and his well-known daughter Pocahontas (Matoaka), were prominent figures in early American colonization history. But the most accessible way to teach their story is the Disney movie *Pocahontas* (Pentecost, Gabriel, & Goldberg, 1995), which teachers can use to activate prior knowledge. To support learning beyond that, educators must dig deeper. Table 4.1 explores possibilities for teaching about Powhatan, Pocahontas, and the Pilgrims.

Sites like Natgeokids.com and AmericanHistoryForKids.com are resources that provide context for textbooks in the form of diverse stories of the people who lived in colonial and precolonial times. Such sites are necessary to provide students with diverse role models.

Many Black students grow up feeling a little ashamed because our part in American history is largely presented as one of defeat and oppression. Finding success stories like those of Black Wall Street in Tulsa or the Harlem Renaissance will give your curriculum balance. Similarly, Hispanic, Indigenous, AAPI, LGBTQ+, and Muslim students also need to see themselves reflected favorably in media and historical contexts to counter a growing acceptance of "inflammatory and divisive rhetoric"

Table 4.1: Powhatan, Pocahontas, and Pilgrims Resource

Grade Level	Discuss	Do	Teach	Reflect
K–2	Indigenous peoples as the earliest inhabitants of North America	Have students trace their family trees going back as far as possible, and then use mathematical estimates to fill in how many great-greats it takes to get back to 1607.	Watch Disney's *Pocahontas*. Then explore the story of the real Pocahontas with a book like *The True Story of Pocahontas: The Other Side of History* (Custalow & Daniel, 2007), written by Indigenous Americans who claim kinship with Pocahontas. Compare and contrast the movie and the book versions.	How was the movie like the real-life story? How was it different?
3–5	Who or what inhabited the Earth sixty million years ago? What about five million years ago? Where did countries and land boundaries come from? What countries existed in the 1600s? Was it OK for some countries to take over land from other countries? Why or why not?	Have students trace their family trees going back as far as possible, and then fill in how many great-greats it takes to get back to 1607. Add a mathematics component to calculate how many generations that would be, based on an average human life span.	Watch *Pocahontas* and then explore the story of the real Pocahontas with a book like *The True Story of Pocahontas: The Other Side of History* (Custalow & Daniel, 2007), written by Indigenous Americans who claim kinship with Pocahontas. Compare and contrast the movie and the book versions. Discuss why the versions are different.	How was the movie like the real-life story? How was it different? How were Indigenous peoples treated? Discuss the Thanksgiving tradition in light of any new information.

continued →

Grade Level	Discuss	Do	Teach	Reflect
6–8	Who or what inhabited the Earth sixty million years ago? What about five million years ago? Where did countries and land boundaries come from? What countries existed in the 1600s? Was it OK for some countries to take over land from other countries? Why or why not?	Have students trace their family trees going back as far as possible, and then fill in how many great-greats it takes to get back to 1607. Discuss whether they had more or fewer great-greats than expected. Discuss why they could or couldn't trace their family trees back to 1607. In light of research results, discuss whether 1607 was a very long time ago or not quite as long ago as they thought.	Watch a clip from *Pocahontas*. Have students research the real Pocahontas, the Powhatan confederation, Chief Wahunsenacawh, and John Smith. Compare and contrast sources and information with the movie. Discuss media literacy and the importance of knowing a writer's perspective and possible intent when portraying history.	Was the movie like the real-life story? What were key differences? How were Indigenous peoples treated? Did Rebecca want to marry John Smith? How old was she?
9–12	Discuss Indigenous peoples as the earliest inhabitants of North America. Discuss the estimated number of tribes or nations before 1607 in what is now known as the United States. Compare and contrast that number to the number of nations and populations in existence today. Discuss possible factors for the decimation of tribes and residual factors caused by traumas like the Trail of Tears. Discuss the current state of diverse Indigenous nations in North America.	Have students research language groups and "pre-contact" maps. Concentrate on the Tidewater region in the Atlantic coastal United States. This area is rich in history from the perspective of both Indigenous peoples and early settlers.	Watch a clip from *Pocahontas*. Have students research the real Pocahontas, the Powhatan confederation, Chief Wahunsenacawh, and John Smith. Contrast the portrayals of stories of the Pilgrims and the Indians with stories about the massacre of 1622.	Was the movie like the real-life story? Did Rebecca want to marry John Smith? How old was she? Do you feel she had the right to say no? Why or why not? Was there gender equality in those times? How fair is the portrayal of "Indians" as the bad guys in early U.S. history? Do prejudices still exist against tribal communities?

Note: This content also appears on https://bedreich.com/blog in a slightly different form.

(Edwards & Rushin, 2018). As research by marketing and economics scholar Griffin Edwards and law scholar Stephen Rushin (2018) bears out, 2016 ushered in "one of the largest upticks in hate crimes in recorded American history." Figure 4.2 provides examples to enrich classroom instruction.

	Names	Impact
Notable Black Americans in History	James Baldwin	Novelist and activist
	Frederick Douglass	Abolitionist and political leader
	Mary McLeod Bethune	Educator and activist
Notable Hispanic Americans in History	Ellen Ochoa	Engineer and astronaut
	Sonia Sotomayor	Associate justice of the Supreme Court
	José Andrés	Chef and philanthropist
	Richard E. Cavazos	Four-star general
Notable Asian Americans in History	Patsy Mink	Attorney and politician
	Kiyoshi Kuromiya	Author and activist
	Chien-Shiung Wu	Nuclear physicist
	Victoria "Vicki" Draves	Olympic gold-medal diver
Notable Muslim Americans in History	Ibtihaj Muhammad	Olympic fencer
	Shaykh Hamza Yusuf	Scholar and activist
	Ilhan Omar	Politician and activist
	Dalia Mogahed	Author and researcher
Notable Indigenous People in History	Mary Golda Ross (Cherokee)	NASA engineer
	John Herrington (Chickasaw)	NASA astronaut
Notable People in History From the LGBTQ+ Community	Josephine Baker	Jazz singer and spy
	Virginia Woolf	Writer
	Bayard Rustin	Civil rights activist
	Pablo Tac (also Indigenous Luiseño)	Linguist and scholar

Figure 4.2: Examples of notable individuals from diverse backgrounds to balance your curriculum.

By remembering how diverse the world is and looking for composers, scientists, writers, and so on from diverse cultures to include in your curriculum, you will mitigate the underlying bias in textbooks toward Eurocentric, White achievement and ensure that all of your students see themselves reflected in their nation's—indeed their world's—rich history.

Fine Arts

Reflect on the phrase *classical music*. Merriam-Webster defines *classical* (n.d.) as "standard" and "of or relating to the ancient Greek and Roman world and especially to its literature, art, architecture, or ideals." If music education is based on Greek and Roman ideals and promotes the contributions of German, Austrian, Russian, and French composers and musicians as the standard, that may leave young musicians from other backgrounds feeling like they belong in a club or at a festival, but not in a concert hall. An online search will render results to help you diversify your list of classical composers. Black composers like Florence Price and William Grant Still, Spanish composers like Santiago de Murcia and Isaac Albéniz, and others such as Louis Wayne Ballard, who was Cherokee-Quapaw, and Gabriela Lena Frank, who is Peruvian, Chinese, Lithuanian, and Jewish, are classical composers who will give a diverse population of music students something to aspire to. Beyond diversifying your list of composers, consider redefining what you actually consider classical (that is, standard, as Merriam-Webster defines it). Latin music, Afro-Caribbean music, and period music from every culture will help to broaden minds and curricula.

While you are looking at composers, also consider the song choices, particularly at the primary school level. Writer Annie Reneau (2020) relates that "standard nursery rhymes most of us recited or sang as children . . . come from racist origins." She also cites The Conscious Kid (2020) on Instagram, who shares a list of offensive songs. Many songs, such as "Five Little Monkeys" and "Ten Little Indians," are rooted in the racist past of the United States and the minstrel days when Whites in blackface performed musical numbers poking fun at Blacks for being uneducated, all while making it illegal for them to get an education. Musicologist Katya Ermolaeva (2019) writes in depth about how the stereotypes passed down in those historically popular songs still have ramifications today because they "conditioned White audiences to believe that African Americans were meant to be physically abused and that their bodies were immune to pain." Although the students who sing these songs are likely not aware of the connection to racism, when they look back at music class with adult understanding, you want to be on the side of history that values and respects diversity, putting away those things that historically caused pain and division in the United States.

Another way to further reduce bias is to vary the order in which you present material to mitigate the subtle but unmistakable "White first" message. For example, in music, consider presenting the works of Mexican composer Gabriela Ortiz before getting to works from European composers to avoid bias based on what communication science scholars Camiel J. Beukeboom and Christian Burgers (2019) call the automatic "content of the cognitive representation [or the ideas that] people hold about a social category" (p. 9). In layman's terms, what is presented first sequentially assumes greater importance in a learner's mind.

Art is also widely taught through the Greco-Roman, "standard" lens, although there are many art styles and periods that both predate classical art that come from all epochs and cultures around the globe. Often, K–12 art teachers look beyond their art history curricula to find artists who more closely reflect their class demographic. According to one art teacher at a North Texas public charter school, teaching a diverse population gave her the impulse to expand her repertoire to also include artists who her "kids would want to learn about" (A. Pace, personal communication, October 26, 2020). Combing the internet for resources using searches like "artifacts from the Kingdom of Benin," "Four Masters of the Ming Dynasty," "components of Islamic art," and so on will allow you to reshape your curriculum into a more inclusive one.

Although, in my experience, theater tends to incorporate more diverse resources, this may not be the case for everyone. When choosing monologues, plays, and University Interscholastic League materials, encourage the exploration of pieces from diverse American classics like those from Ntozake Shange, José Cruz González, and Guillermo Reyes, or check out the selection from the Native American Women Playwrights Archive on Miami University's website (https://spec.lib.miamioh.edu/home/nawpa).

STEM

Rosters of science, technology, engineering, and mathematics greats are also populated by White males, and White males continue to be the largest demographic in the STEM workforce. Figure 4.3 (page 60) shows the disparity between demographic groups in science and engineering careers.

To combat that underrepresentation and build a talent pipeline, projects like the Underrepresentation Curriculum Project (https://underrep.com) and Radical Math (www.radicalmath.org) combine social justice themes with content and are excellent go-to resources to find STEM heroes from various cultures. And if you teach high school juniors and seniors, be aware that there are various tech companies that are actively working to diversify their talent pools by partnering with colleges and universities, particularly historically Black colleges and universities (HBCUs). By visiting UNCF.org, or AnitaB.org, you can find up-to-date partnerships between companies like Amazon, Merck, Zillow, and others, and their work with HBCU students so that these colleges can be on your students' radars.

Employed scientists and engineers	Female	Male
Demographic characteristic (number)	13,720,000	14,907,000
Ethnicity and race (by percentage)		
Hispanic or Latino	10.0	8.5
American Indian or Alaska Native	0.3	0.3
Asian	12.5	14.5
Black or African American	8.3	6.2
Native Hawaiian or Other Pacific Islander	0.2	0.4
White	66.2	68.0
More than one race	2.5	2.1

Source: Adapted from National Center for Science and Engineering Statistics, 2021.

Figure 4.3: The disparity in demographic groups in science and engineering careers.

Finally, if you teach biology or life sciences, you have an excellent opportunity to build projects around race as a social construct. As you talk about DNA, cells, alleles, and dominant and recessive traits, you can solidify the concept that students' universal similarity is greater than their superficial differences since, as Italian researcher Ludovica Lorusso (2011) writes, the "concept of race cannot be established by any ethical argument" (p. 535). Chapter 2 of *What Is Anti-Racism?* (Nichols, 2021), a book I wrote for grades 4–7, is an excellent teaching resource on what race is and isn't. It builds on the work of researchers at the Center for Race and Gender at the University of California, Berkeley. For older students, the Human Genome Project (www.genome.gov/human-genome-project) is an excellent place to start exploring the research outcomes that disprove race as a scientific concept.

English Language Arts

English language arts instruction lends itself easily to integration within other subjects, particularly in the early grades. In addition to using strategies like multilingual vocabulary and think-pair-share activities provided earlier in this book (see Assessment Language, page 41), add diverse literature. We Need Diverse Books (https://diversebooks.org) is an excellent starting place to learn about and order books featuring diverse characters and authors. Additionally, examining popular grade-level reading lists with older students and asking, "Who else was there?" or "Who is missing?" is a great conversation starter for classes looking to explore the intersection of Western classical educational norms and biases. See the activities in the following section for more clarification on using this sort of prompt. Lastly, when teaching writing, especially to students learning English as a second language, cycle back to multilingualism. Encourage students to draft in their first language, if they find it helpful to do so. For native language speakers, encourage using the dump write technique so that students can "dump" ideas onto the page in whatever vernacular or combination of dialects they choose, before translating ideas into academic language.

Learning Together

If you don't feel confident enough to augment your curriculum with additional culturally responsive resources, consider making it a class project. When teaching students of any age, begin by asking them, "Who else do you think was there?" Reading about colonial events and figures? Ask them who were the wives, children, servants, enslaved Africans, or Indigenous nations whose stories might connect to these historical "main characters." Listening to music from the 1920s and looking at pictures of dappers and flappers? Ask who might be missing or what was happening during the same time in other parts of the world. Discussing rail travel? Find out who was building the railway system and building the trains. Try the research activity in figure 4.4 (page 62) to broaden your own knowledge base, or try completing the activity with your students.

Asking yourself and your students, "Who else was there?" is a great way to find little-known historical facts and perspectives. Historical facts and figures that your research uncovers don't have to reinforce your beliefs or ideologies, and not all of them should. Your goal is to fill in the blanks of history without passing judgment. When you read that Thomas Jefferson impregnated his deceased wife's young teenage half-sister, whom he also enslaved, your temptation may be either to cover it up so as not to tarnish the reputation of a Founding Father or to think less of him in his role as a Founding Father. Especially while working with students, resist the temptation to address uncomfortable truths through the lens of your personal belief system. We want to be objective observers of history, as much as lies within us.

Lastly, in all content areas, use your library and search engines to find supplemental material that values contributions from diverse peoples. Once your students are old enough—usually by third or fourth grade—teach them to conduct sound research and pick their own relevant major players. You may need to give certain guidelines to meet academic standards, but try not to impose too many. Great musicians may have to be composers and instrumentalists, but is there any real reason

Famous Historical Person	Who Else Was There	What Was This Person Known For?
Example: Christopher Columbus	Pedro Alonso Niño	Piloted the Santa María; may have been the first to sight land
	The Taíno	The millions of people Columbus encountered
	Friar Ramón Pané	Lived among the Taíno and chronicled their way of life
President Thomas Jefferson	Sally Hemings	
Alexander Graham Bell	Lewis Howard Latimer	
Edward Jenner	Onesimus	
Elvis Presley	Big Mama Thornton	
Martin Luther King, Jr.	Fannie Lou Hamer	

Figure 4.4: Who else was there? activity.

Visit **go.SolutionTree.com/diversityandequity** *for a free reproducible version of this figure.*

why they have to be dead? There is nothing wrong with valuing the living, or at least the more recently dead. Both John Lewis and Neil Armstrong were alive during my lifetime, and they had iconic status while they were living. There is no rule that says one period trumps another. The further along people move through history, the more the status of recent happenings rises, so don't be afraid to mix the new with the old as you broaden your scope on the way to a more inclusive classroom.

Reflection to Action

By now, I will assume that your journal is somewhere close by and that you have already written down some highlights and reflection points from this chapter. Continue your learning and reflection by answering the following questions as honestly and transparently as possible.

1. Do you think there is more to history than what you learned as a child? What kinds of things come to mind when you ask yourself, "Who else was there?"

2. Do you feel that the integration of diverse perspectives in history could be unifying? Why or why not?

3. Have you ever taken a course primarily highlighting the contributions of non-White historical figures? Why or why not?

4.   Do you feel that the Founding Fathers' legacy is diminished as people learn about their slaveholdings or sexual exploits? Can greatness exist in flawed individuals? Why or why not?

In table 4.2 you will again find activities that you can use to share your learning with others.

Table 4.2: Sharing What I've Learned About Representing Diverse Perspectives Through Content and Curriculum

Group	Activity
Littles (preK–grade 3)	Ask, "Who else was there?" For example, when teaching about presidents, research and share facts about their wives and children to build context; or when teaching about Thanksgiving, include the stories of the Wampanoag and other nations already living in what is now the United States when the English came. When teaching about historical events, look for untold stories and unsung heroes, artists, and inventors. Use searches like "unsung heroes of the West" or "diverse inventors."
Middles (grades 4–7)	Use the previous activities. Expand on "Who else was there?" by asking students why they believe some historical perspectives are more prominent and some less prominent or missing altogether.
Secondary	Expand on the previous activities and allow students to build research fluency by having them research "Who else was there?" and "What else was happening?" whenever the opportunity arises. For example, have students research a day, date, or decade in history to find stories beyond the historical headlines they typically learn about. Connect this to media literacy by pointing out that everything, including historical documents, is written by someone with beliefs and ideas of their own, which can influence how they present the facts. Discuss concepts like objectivity, author intent, filter bubble, and implicit bias among historians.
Staff	Use content-team professional development to build a cache of content and standards-aligned resources that answer the question, "Who else was there?" Such resources might include information on people connected to major historical figures like spouses, children, business partners, or rivals. Add the resources to a Wakelet (https://wakelet.com), Padlet (https://padlet.com), or your school's lesson plan hub.
Parents and Community	Share "Did you know . . .?" fun facts in newsletters or other school communication. For example, *Did you know that Mrs. Mary Todd Lincoln overcame struggles with loss and depression? She also supported emancipation in opposition to many Confederate members.* Or, *Did you know that Coretta Scott King was a singer in her early years?* Finally, make families aware of diverse cultural or historical celebrations going on in your area, like Juneteenth or Cinco de Mayo.

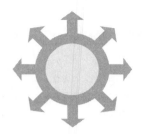

CHAPTER FIVE

Bias and Cultural Expression

During my first year of college, one of the first things I remember learning about in Communications 101 was the term *code-switching*. Suddenly I understood what I'd been doing organically for years. According to University of Michigan researchers Courtney L. McCluney, Kathrina Robotham, Serenity Lee, Richard Smith, and Myles Durkee (2019), code-switching "involves adjusting one's style of speech, appearance, behavior, and expression in ways that will optimize the comfort of others in exchange for fair treatment, quality service, and employment opportunities." The researchers introduce one example of code-switching: a group of Black students who use academic "English in the classroom and African-American Vernacular English (AAVE) with their peers" (McCluney et al., 2019). Another example of code-switching would be Hispanic students speaking Spanish at lunch but not discussing a literary text in Spanish in small groups in class, even when the group consists only of peers who speak Spanish.

Code-switching is something we all do. It's like talking to toddlers versus talking to adults. It's like a preacher's pulpit cadence versus his regular talking voice. It's the switching of hats for formal and informal spaces. Code-switching occurs usually because of negative stereotypes associated with certain modes of expression. Students who speak Spanish or another language other than English may be afraid to be seen as uneducated or even "illegal." Other students might code switch because they are afraid to be labeled as unintelligent, "ghetto," or even criminal because of stigmas surrounding certain types of dress, hair and makeup, or mannerisms. For people who are not a part of the dominant culture, code-switching can mean acceptance or rejection, and it happens almost automatically. In my house growing up, using slang wasn't really permitted, so when I got to be a teenager, I soaked up all the cool phrases. But I learned that cool for my White friends was different than cool for my Black friends, so while I could use all of my cool—which arguably was never much—for my Black friends, that very lack of cool is probably what made me cool to my White friends.

I see the same code-switching in my own students. At recess they listen to the Colombian sounds of cumbia or strains of Mexican norteño and speak Spanish. If I ask them to explain a concept in Spanish in class or if I play cumbia as background music during independent work time, they look taken aback and even ask me why. Without consciously knowing it, they feel they need to be the American kid—whatever that means—in class. They feel, or maybe sense, that their heritage has to be tucked away. Are you giving your students the feeling that they are only accepted when they are assimilated? While teaching academic discourse is appropriate and necessary to prepare students for the global marketplace, it's also important that students feel that expression and language vary according to the setting, and that, while settings change, cultural assertion will always be affirmed—the fifth guiding principle (see figure 5.1).

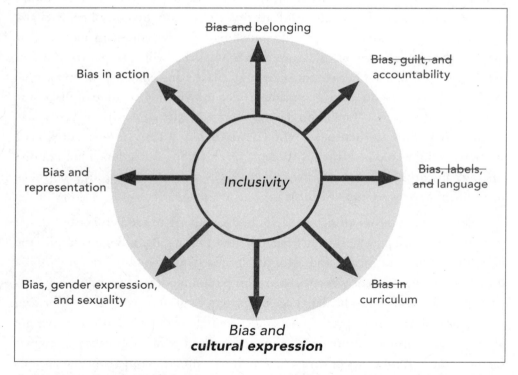

Figure 5.1: Guiding principle 5—Accept diverse forms of cultural expression.

As stated in chapter 3 (page 33), allowing students freedom to discuss texts in their first language can be helpful in reading comprehension. But what about at other times during the school day? What about dialects or other forms of cultural expression? Do the students in your school feel comfortable to code switch between academic and informal communication, languages, and dialects? This chapter explores the intersection of language and cultural expression and provides necessary tools to help you appropriately integrate diverse forms of expression in a classroom setting.

Language as Cultural Expression

While living in Switzerland, especially at first, when I was just learning German, I would have interactions with people who would speak s l o w l y and LOUDLY to me to ensure that I understood them. Not surprisingly, I still didn't understand them. In English, I am a bit of a wordsmith, but in the German part of Switzerland, I fumbled my way through every interaction. Slowly, over years, I mastered the language, but in those early days, I remember seeing eye rolls and frustration in others at my lack of understanding. I was written off as substandard, dumb even, because I didn't know the language. Not knowing the language meant that I was not a part of the culture. For the Swiss, my inability to speak and understand German was irrefutable proof that I didn't belong. As I gained knowledge and confidence in my German language skills, things began to change. Knowing the language was like receiving a key. I went from being limited in my interactions with everyone I encountered to becoming a welcome part of village life. I began to understand and listen to music in the local dialect, and go to comedy shows. I sang their children's songs and read the local news. I stopped on the sidewalk to engage in small talk about local happenings. In short, learning German, particularly the local dialect, gave me inner-circle access to the culture and country. I was no longer the intellectually challenged foreigner they had to shout at.

It may help to think of this type of experience when we meet Spanish-speaking parents, hear our Vietnamese students speak with an accent, or listen to students answering a class question in African American Vernacular English (AAVE). Do we doubt their intelligence or academic ability? Do we assume that they don't belong?

Language and culture are like separate roots of the same big tree. University of British Columbia communications strategist Aubrey N. Leveridge (2008) puts it this way:

> The implications of language being completely entwined in culture, in regards for language teaching and language policy are far reaching. Language teachers must instruct their students on the cultural background of language usage, choose culturally

appropriate teaching styles, and explore culturally based linguistic differences to promote understanding instead of misconceptions or prejudices.

When we realize that language and culture are intertwined, we can avoid placing undue value on linguistic expression, recognizing that we are often measuring someone else by how well they are assimilating into our culture.

Using figure 5.2, reflect on the following scenarios and rate your level of comfort on the Likert scale, with 1 being not at all comfortable and 5 being very comfortable. Make notes in the column, documenting any reasoning or past experiences that might be causal factors for your level of comfort, or write about how you might react in the situation.

Situation	Rating 1: Not at all comfortable 2: Somewhat uncomfortable 3: Neutral 4: Somewhat comfortable 5: Very comfortable	Notes (Why does this make me feel uncomfortable? Have I encountered similar situations previously?)
Walking past a group of students in the hall laughing and speaking in Spanish		
Having a student in a hoodie correctly explain a mathematics problem using slang and colloquialisms, some of which you don't understand		
Having a student give a presentation in another language while her partner translates		
Working on a team with a colleague who has a strong accent		
Talking with parents at open house, several of whom speak other languages and have limited English proficiency		

Figure 5.2: Scenarios and comfort.

Visit **go.SolutionTree.com/diversityandequity** *for a free reproducible version of this figure.*

As you review your notes, reflect on how many of the scenarios are similar to your experiences. If necessary, come up with your own scenarios and triggers. Is there a pattern? Is there a particular trigger that runs, like a red line, through multiple situations? If so, try to find out what that is and how you can work to mitigate your negative reaction. As a start, try to be aware of your triggers so that you can remind yourself to react differently and with more empathy.

Style, Culture, and Discrimination

One other thing I did when I first got to Switzerland was to dress like an American. The Swiss say there is no bad weather, only bad clothes, and that dictates Swiss style, particularly for those living in the provinces, as I did. In addition to learning how to speak the language, I learned how to dress appropriately. I learned that Merrell and North Face trumped Kate and Kors, and that fleece—not a white-collared shirt—was a closet staple. Style in the Alps was much different than what I was used to. Not better, not worse, just different, and I was out of step. That was a realization I came to over time, and yes, I did scoff when I found out that *good shoes* meant sturdy hiking boots. I was encountering an intersection of style and culture that also intertwined with language. But not dissin' somebody's style is about givin' them mad respect for bein' who they are. Notice the voice shift? Did you doubt my ability to communicate appropriately for an academic audience momentarily? If you did, now is a good time to make note of it in your journal so that you can reflect on what those thoughts mean and whether or not you passed judgment on my sudden usage of a different linguistic style.

That's what we do when we scoff at the way others present information, especially if the information is correct and useful. To be judged acceptable in a classroom setting, the expectation is that academic, mainstream-sounding discourse is the norm. For students with an accent or style that does not mimic that of the dominant culture, stereotype threat causes stress: "Students expressed a fear that if they spoke in class in their own discursive styles (their native voices) they would be judged negatively" (White & Ali-Khan, 2013).

Unfortunately, the cultural style with which information is presented can be confused with intelligence or learnedness. This judgment of linguistic mannerisms can be accompanied by judgment of dress, hair, assumed socioeconomic status, and even how we carry ourselves. To illustrate this point, google *Obama walking*. In contrast to *Bush walking*, the search turns up multiple pages of what Michelle Obama calls the former president's "swagalicious" walk (Kimble, 2016). Yes, it may be that people found Barack Obama swagalicious, but it's also likely that having a president walk across the South Lawn with an urban swagger was seen as newsworthy. In this instance, the attention his "urban swag" garnered was positive, but this is not always the case.

Cultural expression should not have anything to do with the quality of education students receive, but it often does. Projects like 56 Black Men (http://56Blackmen .com) from photographer and activist Cephas Williams take an in-depth look at, for example, the Black-man-in-a-hoodie stereotype, but this is only one type of cultural expression that can dangerously and adversely affect students because of its perception. As journalist Sofia Gonzalez (2020) reports, the December 2020 *Vogue* cover of singer Harry Styles wearing a dress prompted strong commentary for and against the style choice from a flurry of news outlets, magazines, and even politicians on what was seen by some as the feminization of men. These are only some forms of cultural expression that can cause bias to interfere with educational outcomes.

Homophobia is a problem for students from sexual minorities in the classroom, as in larger society, and similar to a Black boy in a hoodie, a boy expressing himself in a way that does not conform to heterosexual norms will likely face discrimination that will affect his mental health. The Trevor Project (https://thetrevorproject.org) and the Gay, Lesbian, and Straight Education Network (GLSEN; https://glsen.org) can provide educators with resources and statistics on rates of depression and suicide that plague LGBTQ+ students as well as resources on how to become a more supportive educator for your students from the LGBTQ+ community. The sobering current estimate from the Trevor Project (2021) is that one LGBTQ+ youth attempts suicide every 45 seconds. Style and culture are so integral to how students express themselves and explore their identities, and this intersection can also be a point of vulnerability for marginalized groups. Their identities should not be responsible for poor student mental health outcomes; and we can ensure that they aren't.

Practicing Acceptance With Intentionality

Learning to accept people's differences might seem like a basic good interpersonal skill, but it is not one that comes without practice. Just as people tolerate varying levels of exoticism when it comes to cuisine, people also have varying levels of tolerance when it comes to accepting human differences. Parents know that exposing children to a variety of foods helps them become less finicky eaters; exposing children to different kinds of people early in their lives works the same way and helps them expect the world to reflect the diversity of their early experiences.

In my former life as a music teacher and Grammy-nominated artist, I released a CD called *The Church Bench*. In between tracks of music from my childhood, I talk about my memories of life as seen from the church bench. One of those experiences as a "church baby" was being "passed from hand to hand" on Sundays. Church babies were everyone's child, equally at home in whichever set of caring arms was lovingly pinching cheeks and passing out peppermint candy. There was something good about learning to have positive interactions, no matter how small, with different people in a community. Those were different times, but that feeling of being able to relate to many different kinds of people with warmth and acceptance has stayed.

Luckily, early experience is not the only way people can learn to accept people who may or may not be like them. First, anything you do regularly, you get better at, so be intentional about developing relationships with people who are not like you. As an educator, you may find it hard to find the time, but it is a worthwhile investment that will go a long way in helping you to accept students who are not like you. Start close by. Might there be someone in your own family with whom you can begin building a better relationship? What about your middle sister or a brother-in-law you never got along with? In your intentional relationship building, begin by figuring out what it is about the person that has kept you from having a good relationship. Once you figure out what it is, and why you feel uncomfortable or threatened, work on changing the one person in the relationship you can change: yourself. How can you begin to accept this other person's ideas, ideologies, and what you might call quirks? How can you be transparent and develop a sense of esteem so that this person wants to be in a relationship with you? Being an ally to all your students requires that you are honest with yourself about the messaging you grew up with, the thoughts of friends and family closest to you, the beliefs in your faith community, and what you feel about people but are afraid to say out loud. When you do that, you can examine why you feel the way you do so you can look for ways to build congruence between your ideologies and what you really want for each of your students.

Once you choose someone, you can decide whether or not to communicate your intent, or whether you want to just work on building a better relationship. For example, you can choose to call up your middle sister and say, "Hey, Meredith, I am on a personal growth trip, and we've never really had one of those TV sister relationships, so I'm thinking, could you help me out and we could try to change that?" Alternately, you could simply call up Meredith, ask her to lunch, and go from there.

This might seem like a lot of effort to put into becoming a better educator. But accepting people's varied cultural expressions is simply a matter of finding your triggers and practicing empathy in spite of them. This doesn't mean that you remove boundaries between you and unhealthy or abusive relationships, only that you consider opening a door to a relationship that might enrich both your lives if one of you makes the first step. Starting with someone you're invested in will hopefully make it easy to begin. Use figure 5.3 as a tool to help you not only choose a relationship to work on but also document your learning about acceptance.

Name	Relationship	Quirk or Trigger	Strengths	Changes I Need to Make	Time Spent	Outcome

Figure 5.3: Choose a relationship to invest in.

*Visit **go.SolutionTree.com/diversityandequity** for a free reproducible version of this figure.*

As you learn about being intentional in the way that you accept those who are different from you, concentrating on their strengths will help you to develop a strengths-based lens with which to view others. Having a strengths-based lens means you extend grace and see the positive aspects of people's character as opposed to concentrating on what they need to work on. As clinical psychologist Elsie Jones-Smith (2019) writes, this strength-based lens is commonly used in psychology and social work. Just as psychologists and social workers use a strengths-based approach "to build resilience and to decrease or mitigate trauma within the sociocultural context" (Jones-Smith, 2019, p. 9), relating to people—and students—with your focus on their strengths will reduce discord within the context of your relationship. In short, people who feel valued are more likely to build trusting relationships with those who value them. Sometimes it's just a person's style or mannerisms that irk us, so look for an attribute or accomplishment to compliment or praise, and focus on that.

Once you find your triggers and learn to value character traits that may have been obscured by focusing on another person's perceived deficits rather than valuing that person's strengths, it's time to revisit figure 5.3. What have you learned that you can take into the classroom with you? What kinds of triggers or quirks might be similar to those you experience in the classroom? For example, let's say you are a proud Republican but your brother-in-law is a married, gay Democrat with fairly liberal views. You are both parents, and he works in a nonprofit that supports STEM education initiatives for underserved populations. You may find that by committing to getting to know him, you both have warm and structured parenting styles, he, like you, is a dedicated and faithful partner, and his company helped fund your school's robotics lab. Or you may find that you have very little in common but that your differences make for interesting conversation. The third possibility is that you may come away knowing that you will not become best friends, but you will probably see more reason to value him as a human being and less reason to dismiss him as distasteful and antagonistic.

For you as a teacher, what this all means is that, just like with confronting your brother-in-law, when you confront a student who triggers you for whatever reason, you can:

- Identify and address the trigger
- Make adjustments in your response proactively
- Make it a point to get to know the student personally
- Intentionally find the student's strengths
- Interact with the student from a strengths-based rather than a deficit-based position

When dealing with family, the chances are that culturally you are more likely to be fairly similar. When dealing with twenty to thirty young personalities, the possibilities are endless. Although people all generally want the same basic things as humans, their expressions of those needs and desired ways to meet those needs can differ drastically. Still, using your strengths-based lens, you can meet the challenge of cultural acceptance in your classroom.

Political Acceptance

With Pew Research Center's political polarization trends showing a nation as politically divided as it ever has been (Dimock & Wike, 2020), one of the most common triggers you may encounter in the United States is one of a political nature. Whether you are one lone Democrat in a sea of Republican students or a teacher on a campus as split down the middle as our nation is in 2021, it's a given that you will have to treat "the other side" with respect and esteem at some point.

The first thing you have to do is realize that many people suffer from what political scientists call *affective polarization*, which is the constantly growing dislike and distrust between partisans, such as Republicans and Democrats. Researcher and former ethics educator Paula McAvoy (2016) says that "as our country becomes politically polarized, one effect is that people increasingly distrust—or disdain—those who identify as members of political parties to which they, themselves, do not belong." McAvoy (2016) further asserts that this happens to people regardless of which political party they belong to. Realizing that everyone has a tendency to demonize "the other side" can help people see this as a phenomenon that they have control over. You can examine your own confirmation bias and learn to think more critically about the information you take in regarding those who espouse your beliefs and those who do not. According to the University of Oxford's Catalogue of Bias (Spencer & Heneghan, 2018), *confirmation bias* "occurs when an individual looks for and uses the information to support their own ideas or beliefs" and that further, "individuals then pick out the bits of information that confirm their prejudices." According to accounting and law scholars Benjamin L. Luippold, Stephen Perreault, and James Wainberg (2015), one way to fight your own confirmation bias and be more accepting of other political views is to use an auditor's trick and prove yourself wrong: "Try to disconfirm your initial suspicions by actively seeking out and weighing contradictory information." For example, if you read a headline that demonizes a political candidate you're not fond of, google the person. Look for similarities. Do you both have young children at home? Have you both suffered through a divorce? Did you both play high school soccer? Humanizing people makes it difficult to demonize them. Harvard neuroscience and linguistics student Iqra Noor (2020) notes that another way to fight your own confirmation bias is to "start questioning your research methods and sources used to obtain their information." Use sites like AllSides (www.allsides.com) to compare divergent headlines and increase your own media literacy. Noor (2020) also advocates reading whole articles rather than forming opinions based on headlines. Headlines are designed to grab your attention, and they often use incendiary wording. Reading a whole article instead of just a headline will give you more nuanced and complete information on which to base an opinion.

Confirmation bias is not the only type of bias that prevents people from accepting others and their opinions. Figure 5.4 provides a visual representation of political bias, but these attitudes also factor into nonpolitical othering.

Ideological Acceptance

Often when people discuss mores and ideologies from the perspective of their faith-based value systems, they can forget that there is a separation of church and state. Seeing someone practice a different religion, a different belief, or no faith at all can feel threatening, particularly if you have had negative experiences with people in that group, or if declinism or an availability cascade (see figure 5.4) has already painted a negative picture about a certain group. For example, according to the U.S. Department of Justice (2015), after 9/11, Muslim communities saw an uptick in hate crimes. Similarly, in the political realm, after the 2020 election, episodes of politically motivated violence like those on January 6, 2021, on Capitol Hill have become more commonplace (Bridging Divides Initiative, 2021).

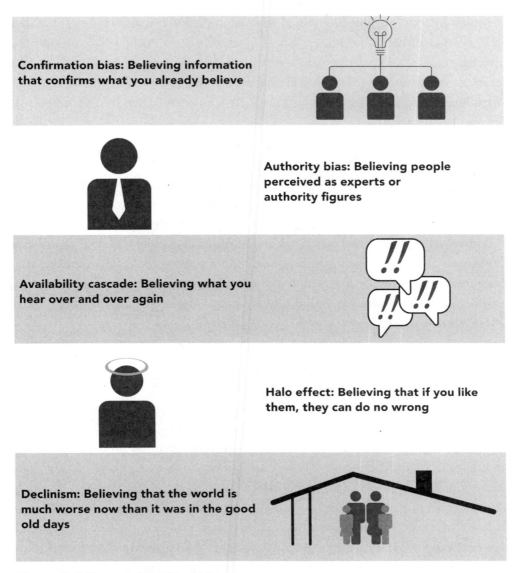

Figure 5.4: Types of political bias.

Teachers can change the trend toward divisiveness by modeling respectful discourse and acceptance. To do that, they need to confront their biases about those who do not share their beliefs. Start by asking yourself how much you know about the ideologies in question. Then think critically about the source of information, as suggested earlier (Noor, 2020). Is it accurate information from a credible source or are you piecing together things you've been told by others? Finally, use figure 5.3 (page 72) to discover your triggers and identify strengths of the other belief system. And remember, people in every political party are trying to do their best for their families. In addition, all major religions have quite a few core principles or values in common, as author and minister Joran Oppelt (2012) points out, like compassion, mutual respect, and treating others in the way we want to be treated. When you examine your perspective on other ideologies, you can intentionally choose to accept what binds you and respect what does not, or at least refrain from being disrespectful in your disagreement.

Cultural Acceptance

With religions and even politics, the sense of being right comes from a place many people consider sacred, but with culture, this feeling of rightness is even more intimate, having to do with your sense of self. As psychology scholar Gwendolyn Seidman (2018) puts it, when you meet someone who is like you, you experience consensual validation. She further explains that "meeting people who share our attitudes makes us feel more confident in our own attitudes about the world" (Seidman, 2018). Since people who are similar validate you, it might be harder to deeply value those who are unlike you.

One way to start practicing cultural acceptance is to give people two gifts: (1) a clean slate and (2) the benefit of the doubt. With a clean slate, you simply tell yourself that whatever you know about a certain group of people is merely propaganda. This person is someone you want to get to know, someone you can learn from, and someone who can help you increase your cultural literacy. The second gift is to give others the benefit of the doubt and assume their intentions are good. Also, assume that none of their differences are there to show you up or diminish you in any way. For example, if your new fifth-grade student happens to be Black and six feet tall, you could forgo any mention of basketball. All tall Black people do not play basketball. Likewise, if a middle school girl gives you "attitude," you could assume that it's not personal and de-escalate the interaction rather than give an office referral. This is hugely important in dealing with Black female students who are at risk because of a disproportionate number of office referrals and exclusionary disciplinary actions. The following scenario illustrates what this might sound like.

Teacher: Jenna, could you please choose a friend to help and pick up the trash around the room?

Student: Why do I have to do it?

Teacher: You don't have to, but I know you're really responsible, and you'll do a good job.

In this scenario, Jenna goes from feeling put upon to feeling empowered. Had the teacher reacted with a stronger directive, he or she could have escalated the situation.

By ignoring the tone Jenna spoke in and encouraging her with a sincere compliment, the teacher averted a power struggle.

As education professor Subini Ancy Annamma and her colleagues (2019) find, the disproportionate number of referrals has little to do with bad behavior and much to do with the fact that U.S. femininity is measured according to middle-class White norms. When they walk into "middle-class white spaces," students of color are considered to be carrying the ghetto with them" and therefore "disproportionate surveillance and punishment often occurs through the application of dominant narratives" (Annamma et al., 2019, p. 213).

When practicing cultural acceptance, it is imperative that you ask yourself by what standards you are judging behavior. This may be where you revisit chapter 1 (page 7) to discover your hidden biases. For example, the first time I took my best friend, who is Catholic, to church with me, she sat, wide-eyed, almost afraid to look around. She described the clapping, the call-and-response cadence of the Baptist preacher and congregation, and the passionate, voluminous strains of the hymns and songs of the choir in two words: loud and long. Likewise, I found the up/down/up/down cadence of the mass I visited with her quiet and short. We both judged the other's church experience by what we knew. However, because we like and respect one another, we accepted each experience as equal. The experiences were new and different but not better or worse than what we knew from our own church experiences.

As teachers, accepting other cultures starts with not judging them by the standard of what we know. Figure 5.5 (page 78) will give you some practice in describing and assigning value to traits. These traits might be ascribed to students or cultures. Only you can decide what they mean to you, and if they convey positive or negative stereotypes. Remember, these are your private notes. Be completely honest so that you can find any blind spots that still need work. Just a note: in my example, I use the word *ghetto*. It's a word I find abhorrent, but to make the point, this will only work if you are being honest with yourself.

If you feel comfortable doing so, you can complete this exercise together with your accountability partner and discuss your answers. Just be aware that if you are sharing this with a person from a marginalized group, you might want to weigh sharing your unfiltered thoughts. Even the best friendship can be taxed by blatant, untempered honesty. So be honest, but choose your words wisely.

Identity Acceptance

If you are somewhere between a Boomer (born 1946–1964) and a Millennial (born 1981–1996), identity, particularly when it comes to gender and sexuality, might not be an explicit concept that you learned about growing up. Shifting to singular *they*

Trait	Description	Association	Negative, Positive, or Neutral	How This Might Influence Cultural Acceptance
Example: Swag	Urban cool or ghetto cool, masculine	Usher; my bestie's boyfriend	Can be positive as in Obama's walk, negative as in gang movie characters, or somewhere in between	There can be something dangerous about that kind of almost bad-boy aura; it could be in an attractive or threatening way. It may affect acceptance and things like police interaction outcomes.
Example: Intelligence	Academic acumen; braininess		Often seen as a positive but might also be viewed as negative, that is, being seen as a know-it-all	
Loudness				
Athleticism				
Sassiness				
Quietness				
Difference				
Bossiness				
Aggressiveness				
Liveliness				
Eloquence				
Nerdiness				

Figure 5.5: Character trait association.

Visit go.SolutionTree.com/diversityandequity for a free reproducible version of this figure.

from *he or she* may ruffle your grammatical feathers, and you may get lost in the number of letters found in LGBTTQQIAAP (lesbian, gay, bisexual, transgender, transsexual, queer, questioning, intersex, asexual, ally, and pansexual). If you are a Millennial or younger, you may feel that your older colleagues are out of touch, caviling, or even homophobic. While there may be truth in any of those statements, the only important truth is that as an educator, your campus should be a safe space for everybody. That means do no harm. Your classroom could be the one place a student feels welcome. According to the National Alliance on Mental Illness (n.d.), in a 2019 survey, "86% of LGBTQ youth reported being harassed or assaulted at school, which can significantly impact their mental health," and the LGBTQ+ community is "one of the most targeted communities by perpetrators of hate crimes in the country."

Whatever you think about identity, gender, and sexuality, your students need you. Sadly, because identity, gender, and sexuality may not present as black and white as being Black and White, some educators choose to ignore their significance. Use the previous tools to combat any biases and then educate yourself. Chapter 6 (page 81) goes into more depth about gender identity and the LGBTQ+ community. If you are a part of the LGBTQ+ community, you might need very different information than a teacher who mentors youth in an evangelical church. Your starting points may be different, and like a Black teacher and a White teacher learning about diversity, your lived experiences may also be different. But the goal is that you can accept and welcome all of your students and their families, regardless of your personal background, beliefs, or preferences.

You can work toward becoming a more inclusive educator by actively making an effort to mitigate your personal biases, developing your cultural literacy, and spending time exploring diverse forms of cultural expression.

Reflection to Action

Once again, take your time and go through the following questions thoughtfully. Use your journal to keep track of anything you want to do further research on. And most of all, be completely honest and transparent with yourself, even if you wish some of your answers were more evolved.

1. What strategies can you easily implement to help you respond more empathetically when you encounter your triggers?

2. Which form of expression do you have the hardest time navigating successfully: linguistic, religious, political, cultural, or identity? Why do you think that is?

3. Who can you talk through your triggers with in at least one of those
    areas, and how can they help you minimize fallout in your interactions?

After reflecting and journaling, you can now consider how you'll share what you've
learned so you can positively impact those around you; table 5.1 includes ideas.

Table 5.1: Sharing What I've Learned About Accepting Diverse Forms of Cultural Expression

Group	Activity
Littles (preK–grade 3)	Learn a song or dance from another culture.
	Have students help decorate for the holidays, especially nontraditional U.S. ones like Chinese New Year, Hanukkah, Kwanzaa, Ramadan, and so on.
Middles (grades 4–7)	Discuss different ways of saying the same thing. Differences could be in word choice, attitude, voice level, or even word emphasis. Discuss how people can misunderstand one another and how to navigate those misunderstandings by asking for clarity and assuming best intent whenever possible.
Secondary	Watch videos of diverse marching bands: U.S. military, European piping and drumming, U.S. college corps bands, U.S. HBCU show bands, Korean marching bands, and so on. Talk about how the different styles are appealing and what aspects students don't like. Make a chart that matches up the plethora of diverse preferences with cultural expressions and discuss what they have in common and how they differ. Discuss also how differences are a matter of taste rather than right or wrong.
Staff	Have a professional development session in which teachers reflect privately on what kinds of cultural displays they find difficult to navigate (such as people who don't celebrate Christmas, "sassy" girls, hijabs, pronouns, and so on). Without going public with reflections, have staff devise and discuss ways to display empathy, especially for those with whom they do not identify.
Parents and Community	Have a communitywide event with diverse food stands to raise money for the school. If your school demographic is homogenous, assign specific countries to classes and have parents prepare and donate dishes from their assigned country's cuisine.
	Send families diverse cultural recipes and world music playlists. Host an in-person or virtual tasting night in which families cook a few simple dishes individually, and then meet up at the school or online at a specified time to try various foods or describe the tastes and textures.

CHAPTER SIX

Bias, Gender Expression, and Sexual Identity

When I was a little girl, my mom was one of the finest gospel choir directors in the country. Because of that, I grew up experiencing a flurry of Sunday night musicals and summer conventions in which all the best choirs would meet up to perform. Those concerts were filled with grand music, colorful robes, and even more colorful people. The male choir directors rarely wore robes. They wore extravagant, well-tailored suits and flashy pocket squares. These men were my mom's peers and close friends, and they formed a close-knit community, a family. My memories of them always bring a smile to my face. They doted on me at restaurants after the concerts, showed me riffs on the piano, and even helped me learn to drive. They were a huge part of my single mom's village.

At some point I realized they were gay. Not all male choir directors are gay, but the ones in my community at that time were, and finding out was inconsequential, like finding out someone's middle name. I never thought much about it until I started paying attention to condemning sermons in the 1980s. I could never figure out how one could hire the best out-and-proud musician for the choir but lambast the gay community from the pulpit. Seeing people I loved experience public rejection like that made me aware of the kind of bias and hypocrisy that is responsible for so much unnecessary pain. Church isn't the only place it happens.

As discussed in the previous chapter, sexual minorities regularly experience rejection and hate, and this often begins within the school community. According to education researchers Joseph P. Robinson and Dorothy L. Espelage (2012), LGBTQ+ youth "experience higher rates of victimization by bullying than do their hetero-sexual-identified peers" (p. 309). This victimization is associated with a number of negative outcomes, including but not limited to "elevated risks for suicide attempts and skipping school out of fear" (Robinson & Espelage, 2012, p. 316).

Further, according to Robinson and Espelage's (2012) research, these outcomes persist even when schools have anti-bullying policies and protections in place, because of the "stigmatizing, macro-level messaging about sexual minority youth that persist even in the absence of direct individual-level peer victimization" (p. 316). In plain language: unless educators want their students to suffer negative outcomes, they need to address the unwillingness or inability of school staff to confront sexual minority equity issues in a knowledgeable and inclusive way. The sixth guiding principle, accept diverse forms of gender expression and sexual identity, reflects this need, as shown in figure 6.1.

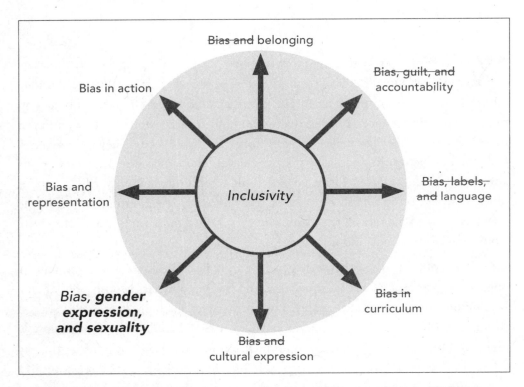

Figure 6.1: Guiding principle 6—Accept diverse forms of gender expression and sexual identity.

In this chapter, I'll discuss some ways to gather knowledge that will help you better understand and support students, colleagues, and parents from the LGBTQ+ community. I will also explore how those of you who are members of this community can navigate the biased behaviors and actions of others.

Gathering Knowledge

Most people who are confronted with something they did not grow up experiencing need at least some time to accept and adjust to someone else's normal. Being around Black people was always my normal. For my teachers, it probably took some getting used to. Similarly, there may be educators who have little or no experience with sexual minorities. If you are knowledgeable and not new to the LGBTQ+ community, I will ask you to be mindful of that fact. Alternately, if you are struggling with ideologies and perhaps faith issues, I will ask you to be mindful of the fact that most major religions call for people to judge their own actions, not those of others. Let's all be mindful of the fact that as educators, our main responsibility is to educate and prepare our students for a successful future; that begins with making sure that all of our students feel accepted. In that spirit, let's go over tools to learn more, as well as definitions and further reading.

Know, Want to Know, Learned (KWL)

Just as educators question students to find out what they know before starting a new unit, they also need to ask themselves questions to find their starting place. In learning how to support students and families from the LGBTQ+ community, you can turn to a tool you might be familiar with: the know, want to know, and learned (KWL) chart (Ogle, 1986), which is an excellent way to clarify where you stand, what you know, and what your action steps will be. I began using this expanded version of KWL in my classrooms in 2018. In the version I've adapted, I find it's helpful to add the following considerations.

- *H*: How do I want to learn something?

- *A*: What actions do I anticipate taking based on what I've learned?

- *Q*: What new questions have I come up with based on what I've learned? (an important question, since learning is always cyclical)

These additions turn the tried-and-true KWL chart into a more open-ended process that gives not only a starting point but also a pathway forward to action and further learning. Use figure 6.2 (page 84) to start your personalized journey into becoming more responsive to the needs of the LGBTQ+ youth you encounter. A tool like this is useful for educators seeking to better understand and support any community of which they are not part, but I have designed this one specifically with the LGBTQ+ community in mind.

K	What do I think I know? What are my current thoughts, feelings, and biases about the LGBTQ+ community?	
W	What do I want to know to become a better practitioner and to be better able to support students and colleagues from the LGBTQ+ community?	
L	What is the most valuable thing I have learned so far? What other supporting findings have I gained understanding about?	
H	How will I find out what I need to know beyond this book?	
A	What actions can I take now to create a more LGBTQ+-inclusive climate? What long-term action can I commit to?	
Q	What new questions do I have, and where can I find answers?	

Figure 6.2: KWL adaptation to support LGBTQ+ students.

What did you learn about yourself and your thoughts surrounding LGBTQ+ issues and concerns? Are you knowledgeable and open to learning more? Are you new to LGBTQ+ concepts but open to creating an inclusive environment for all students? Do you struggle with sexual minority ideologies but are concerned that your personal ideology could cause your students to feel rejected? Are you resistant to the concept of anything other than heteronormative, cisgender identity expressions?

Definitions

Before going any further, it is imperative to have up-to-date and respectful terms for creating a dialogue around gender identity and sexual orientation. It may feel like there are a lot of terms to learn, but that's because the LGBTQ+ term itself encompasses an extremely wide range of expression. Listed in table 6.1 are some of the more common terms you may encounter as you become more culturally aware.

Table 6.1: Key Terms in the LGBTQ+ Community

Term	Definition
Ally	A person supportive of another community; for example, the LGBTQ+ community
Cisgender; cis	People whose gender identity and expression match their birth sex
Coming out	Acknowledgment and disclosure of sexual or gender identity
Deadnaming	Calling transgender people by the name they were assigned at birth rather than the name they currently identify with
Gay	A person romantically and sexually attracted to someone of the same sex; can also be used by nonbinary people

Gender dysphoria	Psychological distress resulting from an incongruence between gender identity and birth sex
Gender expression	The way gender is expressed through dress, mannerisms, or other social signals
Gender identity	A personal concept of gender that can be male, female, neither, or both
Homophobia (also transphobia, biphobia)	Fear of or discomfort with same-sex attraction or people who espouse same-sex attraction (or of transgender or bisexual people)
Homosexual	An offensive term used to describe gay men and women
Lesbian	A woman romantically and sexually attracted to other women; a gay woman
LGBTQIA (also LG, LGBT, LGBTQ+)	An acronym for lesbian, gay, bisexual, transgender, queer or questioning, intersex, asexual or ally; can be shortened or lengthened, hence the +
Misgendering	Using the wrong pronoun to describe a transgender or gender-fluid person
Nonbinary	A person who identifies as neither male nor female and may identify as another gender, both genders, or no gender at all (see TGD)
Outing	Revealing a person's sexual or gender identity without permission; an act of aggression, or when done online, cyberbullying
Sexuality	A composite of a person's biological sex, who a person is physically and romantically attracted to, and what gender a person self-identifies as
Sexual orientation	Identification based on romantic or sexual attraction (such as gay, straight, asexual, bisexual, and so on)
Straight	A commonly used term for a person attracted romantically and sexually to the opposite sex; heterosexual
TGD	Transgender and gender diverse; see nonbinary. Other similar terms include genderqueer, enby ("NB"), genderfluid, agender, and two spirit
Transgender	A term for people whose internal sense of gender identity does not align with their birth sex; may involve social, physical, or medical adaptation

Sources: APA, 2018; coming out, n.d.; Gay and Lesbian Alliance Against Defamation, n.d.; Johns Hopkins University, n.d.; LGBT Foundation, n.d.; Montz, 2019; Trevor Project, n.d.; University of California San Francisco LGBT Resource Center, n.d.

There are other terms and definitions, but these will help you arm yourself with the basic knowledge you need to better relate to students, parents, and peers from the LGBTQ+ community. If you are not familiar with the LGBTQ+ community, some of the terms may seem foreign and that's OK. What's important is that as an educator, you know enough to support your students and families from the LGBTQ+ community.

Further Reading

Finally, because we all still need to learn, table 6.2 provides reading material to support learning. Although it is highly unlikely that literature from one group will appeal to every group, this list attempts to present diverse thought groups with a starting point.

With regard to accepting others in all their diversity, it falls to you to find out what stops you from being empathetic and inclusive, and change it. Use the tools in this chapter and cycle back to them whenever you become aware of a wall going up between you and your students.

Peers and Parents

Although this book primarily talks about interactions with students, it is important, and even perhaps easiest, to interact, learn with, and learn from other adults. Adult interactions are presumably less complex because there are fewer power dynamics in play, which makes mistakes less high stakes. The first thing you can do is to make sure you are part of an LGBTQ+-friendly team, because policy still has a long way to go to become inclusive in all fifty states. The Movement Advancement Project (n.d.) has several infographics, such as the one shown in figure 6.3 (page 88), that give insight on the state of LGBTQ+ equality.

But while policy is changing, you can model acceptance and inclusivity right away. Being the only out gay person on staff is like being the only man or Black person on the team. The possibility exists that you don't quite fit in. Since most cisgender, heterosexual people expect that others are cisgender and heterosexual, people from the LGBTQ+ community are often left with the choice to either be "the gay person" on the team or hide who they are. If the teacher down the hall suddenly appears wearing a two-carat diamond, most people would assume that she's engaged to a man. While statistically speaking, that may be true, if she's in fact engaged to another woman or nonbinary person, avoiding that assumption means you won't be avoiding her for the rest of the week because of some awkward comment you made.

Maybe you are thinking that you don't work with anyone from the LGBTQ+ community. You aren't alone. One out of two heterosexual employees in a Human Rights Campaign (2018) survey believe that they only work with heterosexuals. Further, 46

Table 6.2: LGBTQ+ Learning Resources

If You Are . . .	Read This	Or This
A member of the LGBTQ+ community	The Human Rights Campaign's Welcoming Schools project (http://welcomingschools.org /resources/challenging-questions) helps teachers answer questions and explore gender and sexuality in age-appropriate ways.	*Whosoever* (https://whosoever.org/?s=lgbtq) is a Christian online magazine for Christian members of the LGBTQ+ community looking for faith-based literature and acceptance.
An ally of the LGBTQ+ community	The Human Rights Campaign's Welcoming Schools project (https://welcomingschools.org /resources/challenging-questions/) helps teachers answer questions and explore gender and sexuality in age-appropriate ways, whether you are a member of the community or not.	LGBTQ+ resources for youth are available from the Centers for Disease Control and Prevention (https://cdc.gov/lgbthealth/about.htm). Be informed; be armed with resources. You may be the person your student comes out to.
Only marginally familiar with the LGBTQ+ community	Learning for Justice's LGBTQ+ best practices guide (https://bit.ly/3pXXs7l) is a one-stop-shop resource for educators with curriculum resources, social-emotional learning resources, and additional information to help you learn about the LGBTQ+ community.	*I Am Jazz* (Herthel & Jennings, 2014) and *Being Jazz* (Jennings, 2016) are children's and young adult books from activist and YouTube personality Jazz Jennings. They can help you put a human face and story to the terms and ideologies you're learning about.
Unfamiliar with the LGBTQ+ community	The Human Rights Campaign's *All Children—All Families: Beginner's Guide to LGBTQ Inclusion* (https://bit.ly/2Twpaf6) is a place to begin learning about the LGBTQ+ community and how to create a welcoming environment for sexual minorities.	Safe@School (https://bit.ly/3iQVLqq) is a Canadian program designed to provide strategies for positive action.
Unfamiliar with the LGBTQ+ community with a strong evangelical background	Pastor Nathan Albert's (2016) *Embracing Love: My Journey to Hugging a Man in His Underwear* explains how churches can be more welcoming, making all people, including the LGBTQ+ community, feel like they belong.	"How Should Christians Respond to Gay Friends or Family Members?" (Biola Magazine Staff, 2015) is an interview with the author of the book *Messy Grace: How a Pastor With Gay Parents Learned to Love Others Without Sacrificing Conviction* (Kaltenbach, 2015). For those struggling with LGBTQ+ concepts from a faith stance, this resource offers practical strategies from an evangelical point of view for valuing and respecting people. Muslims for Progressive Values (www.mpvusa.org/lgbtqi-resources) does the same with a Muslim perspective.

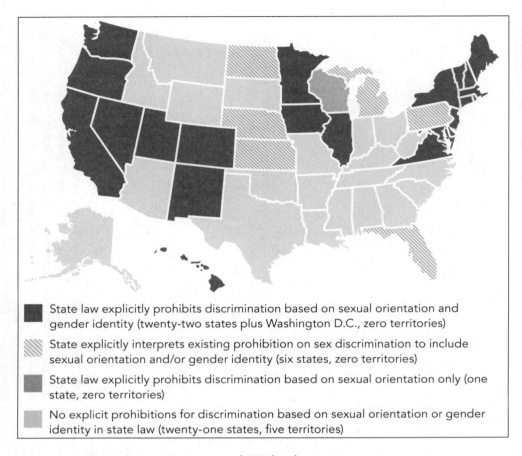

Source: Movement Advancement Project, n.d. Used with permission.

Figure 6.3: Nondiscrimination laws.

percent of LGBTQ+ workers are closeted on the job because of fear of discrimination, making others feel uncomfortable, or losing connections and friends (Human Rights Campaign, 2018). Armed with that knowledge, you can use figure 6.4 for ideas about ensuring an LGBTQ+-friendly culture at your school.

Finally, just remember that people deserve a space in which they have privacy and one in which they feel comfortable enough to be their authentic selves. If you are lucky enough to know how it feels when you are in a space like that, be sure to provide that for others by showing empathy and being inclusive and accepting of others.

These considerations are equally important when interacting with parents. When you are working with parents from the LGBTQ+ community, you are working with parents, period. According to the American Academy of Child and Adolescent Psychiatry (AACAP; 2019), research shows that children with gay and lesbian parents are as well-adjusted as children with heterosexual parents, and it's unfortunate

Things to Say	Things to Do	Things to Avoid
"Oh wow, you're engaged!"	Invite partners whenever spouses are welcome.	"Oh, you're engaged! What's [his or her] name?" (Avoid assuming the gender of a partner.)
"Hey, a couple of us are going for a spa day. Join us?"	Ensure that all teachers are welcome to join after-school activities.	Don't assume certain activities are too masculine or too feminine.
"Oh, I'm sorry. I didn't know your partner was not a man. Please forgive me for assuming."	Apologize for any missteps and move on.	Don't avoid the person out of embarrassment.
"Hey, a couple of us are getting together to choose some more inclusive books for the library. Have any good suggestions?"	Include diverse voices when choosing books, materials, and activities.	"Hey, why do gays _____?" (Using your "one gay friend" as the LGBTQ+ expert is inappropriate and burdensome. Lumping people in the LGBTQ+ community into one group that has the same opinion on everything is also a no-no.)

Figure 6.4: Ways to ensure an LGBTQ+–friendly culture.

that we need research to confirm that. They also report that children from LGBTQ+ parents "can face some additional challenges" (AACAP, 2019). That's where educators come in. According to the AACAP (2019), it's the school environment, not the home environment, that makes things difficult.

How we interact with our parents always has an influence on student well-being and success. According to Abner Oakes (2013), director of outreach for the Institute for Student Achievement, "Successful collaborative relationships with families are based on a number of beliefs about families and the perceived benefits of family-school relationships." When the parent-teacher relationship is a positive, respectful one, students benefit. That means that educators need to have the same baseline belief for all parents, which is that they are providing the best environment that they can for their children.

When two dads come for open house, other parents and students will follow your lead. In my experience, if I welcome them warmly, the same way I do more "traditional" families, the school community will welcome them warmly as well. If you live in a conservative community, this will be especially important and will go a long way toward setting the tone and reducing bullying. The research is clear that the presence of adults who are supportive of LGBTQ+ students and families can have a positive effect on the school experiences of all students and their psychological well-being: "The number of supportive educators was one of the stronger predictors of a less hostile school climate and of greater self-esteem for LGBT students" (Kosciw, Palmer, Kull, & Greytak, 2013, p. 58).

Figure 6.5 provides a list of things you can do to help support your LGBTQ+ families.

Supporting LGBTQ+ Students in the Classroom

Although having students who are open about being a part of the LGBTQ+ community may be new, having gay, questioning, and gender diverse students is not. There have always been students from sexual minorities in schools, and unfortunately, these students have hidden out of fear and shame; often they still do. As with any minority, sexual minorities have civil rights protections, but they deserve more than a school in which they are just not bullied. A hostile environment is not only one in which there is bullying. A lack of acceptance is also hostile, and it disrupts a student's sense of belonging. As an educator, your job is to make sure that each student feels welcome. One way you can embrace your students from the LGBTQ+ community is to ensure that they have representation in the books and media they read and watch. That means including LGBTQ+-friendly media in your libraries, read-alouds, and curriculum. If you are in a school in which materials are controlled or censored, ensure that students know how they can access diverse books and media online or through the public library.

Table 6.3 (page 92) includes suggested books and media for various grade levels. These are only a few of the titles that will allow your students to see themselves reflected. Make sure that you have—or at least know about—not only books that represent diverse sexual minorities but also books that feature protagonists from diverse cultures, like *If You Could Be Mine* from Sara Farizan (2013) or *More Happy Than Not* from Adam Silvera (2015), both young adult titles, or for the littles, *Julián Is a Mermaid* by Jessica Love (2016). In addition to books, be sure to talk about diverse writers, politicians, inventors, musicians, and so on who are also members of the LGBTQ+ community. The important thing is, especially if you have not had much exposure to the LGBTQ+ community or if you have personal feelings that may translate to non-acceptance for your students, to make sure to practice conversations and possible scenarios with a friend or colleague beforehand. Remember, *your personal feelings in a classroom are not the priority*, those of your students are, and

What You Can Do	Why It Will Help
Don't assume people's relationships to one another. Learn and use the phrase "And you are . . .?"	You will avoid embarrassing missteps like saying, "So, is this your sister?" when speaking to a mom about the second mom.
Don't press for relationships during introductions.	If someone introduces oneself only by name, it's not necessary to know the person's relationship to the student. Assume any adult at school and in your records is a valuable part of the student's village.
Prepare your class with books or talks about diverse types of families.	Discussing different types of families will give you a chance to answer questions before those honest, awkward questions come up in a room full of parent-teacher association members and students. If your district prohibits conversations about diversity, use pictures and questioning to get students talking, reflecting, and asking their own questions. Answering student questions can be viewed differently from introducing "controversial" topics.
Consider having an inclusion statement in your school handbook.	Some people may not think beyond a male-female or single-parent household. Giving them the chance to consider other family models *and* know that your school practices inclusion and acceptance sets up your school community as an empathetic and tolerant one.
Be prepared for awkwardness.	If you've never stood next to a small child asking why the lady ahead of you is so fat, you have not experienced the "joy" of childhood honesty. "Why do you have two dads?," "Where's your mom?," or "Are you a boy or a girl?" may be expressed loudly at open house. Be prepared with brief, clear, age-appropriate answers. The less flustered you act, the sooner those moments will become normal. Simple answers work best: • "Some families have two dads; some have no dads. Some have grandmas; some have caring adults and no moms or dads. Families can be pretty different!" • "Billy doesn't have a mom; he has a baba." • "Alex isn't a boy or a girl; they're just Alex."

Figure 6.5: Things you can do to help support your LGBTQ+ families and students.

empathy should be one of the highest priorities in any classroom. Figure 6.6 (page 93) gives some examples of how you can introduce books, lessons, or people and how to react to awkward or uncomfortable questions and responses.

As you gain knowledge and confidence, you will find your own authenticity in empathetically and respectfully answering questions posed by others in your learning community.

Table 6.3: LGBTQ+-Friendly Book and Media Recommendations

Author	Title	Recommended Grade Level
Jessica Walton (2016)	*Introducing Teddy: A Gentle Story About Gender and Friendship*	PreK–K
Justin Richardson and Peter Parnell (2005)	*And Tango Makes Three*	PreK–K
Maya Gonzalez and Matthew SG (2019)	*They, She, He Easy as ABC*	PreK–1
Theresa Thorn (2019)	*It Feels Good to Be Yourself: A Book About Gender Identity*	PreK–3
Rebecca Sugar (2013–2019)	*Steven Universe* (television series)	3–6
Lisa Bunker (2017)	*Felix Yz*	5–8
Ginny Rorby (2019)	*Freeing Finch*	5–9
Sarah Prager (2017)	*Queer, There, and Everywhere: 23 People Who Changed the World*	Young adult

Members of the LGBTQ+ Community

Up until this point, this chapter has addressed those who are outside of the LGBTQ+ community. This section largely addresses educators from the LGBTQ+ community. If you are living as an out LGBTQ+ educator, you don't need advice from a cisgender, straight female educator. However, I know there are many educators who have not yet navigated the often still murky waters of coming out at work, so with a little help from friends from the LGBTQ+ community, I will give you some examples of the kinds of responses you can use in case you are confronted with awkward or even rude questions. If you are not a part of this community, please read on in order to learn what kinds of things you should avoid saying.

First and foremost, wherever you are in your journey as an educator from the LGBTQ+ community, let me challenge you to model the empathy you desire. It isn't easy to educate people all the time or to have to be the bigger person when dealing with wearying microaggressions and discrimination. As a Black woman, I know that it does not matter how many laws change; racism still exists. There will always be anti-Black sentiment, and there will always be anti-LGBTQ+ sentiment and othering of every kind. I cannot change the way people respond to me or "my kind," but

What to Introduce	Possible Question or Comment	How to Respond
"Today we're reading a book about a famous writer from the LGBTQ+ community."	"What's LGBTQ+?"	"That stands for lesbian, gay, bi, transgender, and queer or questioning."
"Let's read *Julián Is a Mermaid* (Love, 2018), a book about a boy who loves dresses."	"Boys don't wear dresses." or "Boys shouldn't wear dresses."	"Many don't, but there are lots who do." or "Why not? Who makes up the ideas about clothes being for a girl or a boy anyway? As long as clothes cover the important parts, why should it matter?" or "Julián feels more like himself in dresses, and we should not look down on others for making different choices."
	"My dad says that boys who wear dresses are gay."	"Some of them are; some of them aren't. We shouldn't label people in any way that makes them feel bad."
	"My church says gay people are going to hell."	"I'm pretty sure God does not need us to tell people where we think they are going when they die. And I'm 100 percent sure he doesn't like it when we are mean to others because they are different."
"Class, these are Jenna's moms. They are talking to us today about careers in medicine."	"How can Jenna have two moms? Doesn't there have to be a dad?"	"There has to be a man to make a baby, but parents can be a mom and dad, two moms, two dads, any combination of these, or none of these."
"Does everyone know what this rainbow lanyard and badge mean?"	"No, what does it mean?"	"This symbolizes that my classroom is a safe space for all students, and it lets my students from the LGBTQ+ community know that they can count on me for support."
	"Rainbow means gay, right?"	"Sort of. It is the symbol of the LGBTQ+ community."
	"You're gay?"	"Yes, I am." or "I'm not, but I am an ally. I believe people have the right to express who they are freely and without judgment."

Figure 6.6: Introducing and responding to questions about the LGBTQ+ community.

I can change the way I respond. Similarly, as a member of a sexual minority, the only reaction you really have control over, no matter how much you desire it to be otherwise, is your own.

Before responding, however, remember that ignoring is also an option. Stop, reflect, and, as writer and producer Andrew Limbong (2020) writes, "Set realistic expectations of what you want from these conversations. . . . It's important to acknowledge that no one is going to learn everything in one conversation overnight." If you decide that it's a conversation you want to have, consider your role and the role of the person you're considering responding to and any possible fallout.

As you have probably learned, the best way to meet comments, slights, or awkward questions is to assume naivete and best intent, at least until you see a recurring pattern of offensive behavior. When you assume best intent, you can gently correct objectionable behaviors. Let's assume that teachers on your staff are beyond "you all" and "all of you" monolithic assumptions and that the kinds of microaggressions you may experience are more subtle. That's more likely to be the case because teachers often have little or no training or experience in how to support students from the LGBTQ+ community. According to Edutopia editor and journalist Emelina Minero (2018), research shows that "teachers reported feeling uncomfortable talking to their students about sexuality due to their beliefs or perceptions about what's appropriate—often conflating sexual orientation with sex—while others felt pressure from administrators or parents to keep tight-lipped."

Questions and comments may come from a lack of knowledge or experience, and although you may feel like you have to do the heavy lifting involved in helping educators become more inclusive, teaching is better than just letting it go, especially considering the impact you will be making on your campus.

Unfortunately, many people still have reason to fear unpleasant consequences or backlash when they discuss any facet of being a part of the LGBTQ+ community. If you, as a lesbian, gay, bisexual, trans, or queer educator, are considering talking to your coworkers or administrators about being a member of the LGBTQ+ community—or if it comes up without you having the opportunity beforehand to frame it in a way that makes you feel safe—figure 6.7 might provide you with some support. The answers use language that displays empathy for a person's possible lack of knowledge while ensuring an opportunity for those you're talking with to reflect on their biases against, or even lack of respect for, sexual minorities.

Additionally, you may receive questions of a personal or sexual nature or even questions about your stage of transitioning if you are transgender. When this happens, don't feel obligated to share more information than you want to. If what you

Comment or Question	Response
"Oh, so you have a wife?"	"Yes." Then move on.
"What do your students think when they see your wedding picture? Isn't it confusing?"	"Not at all. Children are naturally inclusive until they are taught not to be. Would you and your students like to join us for a read-aloud of *I Am Jazz*?"
"So, have you ever been with a [man or woman]?" or "When did you find out you were gay?"	"Will you change your opinion of me or judge me depending on my answer? Why do you ask?"
"So, your wife, what's *she* like?"	"My wife is great! They're a pretty awful cook, but they have a sense of humor to make up for it! Maddie uses the pronoun *they* instead of *she*."
"But then, I guess you don't go to church."	"Why would you guess that?" or "My husband and I are active in our church. That's where we met."

Figure 6.7: Responding in awkward moments.

want to share is nothing, that's OK too. In the same way that I set boundaries with strangers who want to touch my hair or ask me if it's "all mine," it's OK to tell someone that you find the questions overly personal, without justifying your reason for not answering.

If you find people being rude to, misgendering, or deadnaming you or other members of the LGBTQ+ community, then it's time to remind them that if they want to have empathetic students, they should model that empathy; whether or not they do, you can. You will never win acceptance from everyone, and that should not be the goal. The important thing about your presence on campus is that you will be able to empathize with students being othered, especially those from the LGBTQ+ community. You can be a role model, whether you are a silent warrior or a vocal advocate.

Reflection to Action

By now, you are a pro at knowing what to do here. I hope that you have already made notes in your journal to help you connect what you've learned to your own prior knowledge. As you answer the following questions, consider not only the questions themselves but what it means to be a part of a marginalized community or an ally to a marginalized community.

1. If I am uncomfortable with people from the LGBTQ+ community, how can I become less awkward and more accepting in my interactions?

2. If I am from the LGBTQ+ community, what are my triggers when I respond to microaggressions or even curiosity?

3. What resources or organizations can provide guidance and information to help me better support my students?

Once you've reflected and journaled, the activities in table 6.4 will allow you to move from reflection to action in your learning community. You don't have to use all of the activities with all your groups, or eat the whole elephant at once. Remember, small bites.

Table 6.4: Sharing What I've Learned About Accepting Diverse Forms of Gender Expression and Sexual Identity

Group	Activity
Littles (preK–grade 3)	Ask students, "What is a family?" and "Is everyone's family the same? How are our families the same? How are they different?" Have a student inquiry–guided conversation in which you give prompts and ask questions, rather than leading a class discussion.
	Write various class duties or jobs over Venn diagrams labeled boy, girl, and neutral. This can be done on a Zoom whiteboard, a class whiteboard, with chalk outside, or even using polling instead of diagrams. Have students write or draw a predesignated symbol for boy, girl, and neutral under each job. When the Venn diagrams are done, have a discussion about gender stereotypes and, for example, whether all firefighters are indeed men.
Middles (grades 4–7)	Talk about the history of the rainbow flag. Discuss discrimination, empathy, and the need for nonjudgmental inclusion of all identity groups.
	Watch this Welcoming Schools video (https://youtu.be/tjYTAGZgl7o) with your students and discuss how to choose words that help, not hurt.
Secondary	Talk about the history of the rainbow flag, the letters LGBTQIA+, and the need for respectful discourse so that people from the LGBTQ+ community feel safe and welcome.
	Discuss the difference between tolerance, acceptance, and inclusion. What does it feel like to be tolerated? What does it feel like to be included? Have a student lead the discussion after setting ground rules for respectful discourse.

Group	Activity
Staff	Watch this video: https://welcomingschools.org/resources/what-i-need-to-succeed-at-school-video Then, make any necessary changes to your handbook so that students and families from the LGBTQ+ community feel safe.
Parents and Community	With 5.6 percent of the U.S. population identifying as LGBTQ+, it's important to recognize that on average, one out of twenty people is a part of the LGBTQ+ community (Miller, 2021). As you make your schools safe places for all, provide clarity to families, letting them know that empathy, respect, and acceptance are non-negotiables. Consider including a link to the Welcoming Schools video from the previous row in a newsletter.

CHAPTER SEVEN

Bias and Representation

During a professional development session I attended, teachers asked if celebrating months—National Native American Heritage Month, Black History Month, Hispanic Heritage Month, and so on—was being culturally responsive. If you're like most teachers, you would probably answer *yes*, as they did. I decidedly did not answer *yes*; marginalizing the stories of a cultural group eleven months out of the year is certainly *not* culturally responsive. While the intent behind these designated months is good, it is a practice that celebrates the superior position of a dominant culture by making outliers of the groups that do not belong to the dominant culture. There's history, and there's Black history; there is heritage, and there is Hispanic heritage; and there's the story of Plymouth Rock, and there's the story of the Wampanoag. The problem is that all these stories are American history. If educators are being culturally responsive, the various stories and perspectives of the inhabitants of America should all be a part of the daily curriculum.

That's not to say that these designated times are completely without value. Months celebrating diversity have been a good place to start, especially for a country unused to multiperspectivity. The tradition began with Negro History Week in February 1926, a week dedicated to the study of the Black past, started by Carter G. Woodson. His idea was to focus on the "countless black men and women who had contributed to the advancement of human civilization" (Scott, 2011). But alongside this focus, he cautioned against ignoring Black stories during the rest of the year; he advocated that the achievements of Black people be taught in schools and communities throughout the year, not only in February. A time of celebration of Black achievement would not be recognized by the government for another fifty years when Black History Month became official (Scott, 2011).

Hispanic Heritage Month was made official in 1988 (National Hispanic Heritage Month, n.d.), and that opened gates to months celebrating Indigenous people, Asian people, Pacific Islanders, Jewish people, women, and the LGBTQ+ community. No doubt there are more to follow. However, maybe before you fill your calendar, you can fill your classroom, campus, and curriculum with celebrations of diversity in ways that equitably honor everyone's stories every day. That's why the seventh guiding principle is to ensure representation throughout the year, not just during designated months, as shown in figure 7.1.

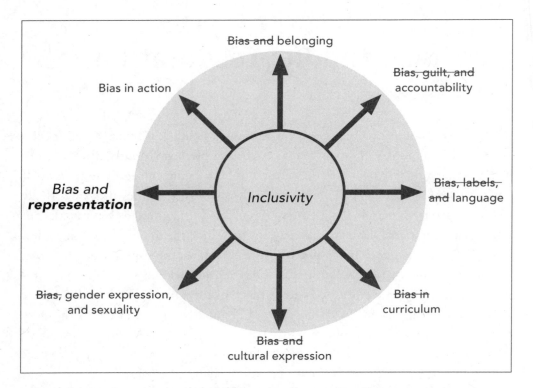

Figure 7.1: Guiding principle 7—Ensure representation throughout the year, not just during designated months.

In chapter 4 (page 49), you learned that there are many ways to ensure that your students see themselves represented through reading, learning, and play materials. You also learned how to incorporate first-person stories and stories of unsung heroes in your curriculum. However, representation goes even beyond that. Chapter 7 goes further to discuss a number of ways to make sure representation is a focus throughout the year. Getting to know your students, helping your students get to know each other by celebrating their individual diversity and practicing how to debate and disagree, and helping them master content through a cultural lens are all ways you can put the focus on diversity and inclusivity.

Get to Know Your Students

Who are your students? What do they enjoy? What do they dislike? Where are their parents from? What traditions are important to them? By getting to know your students, you will discover unique opportunities to find out what's important to them and build an ongoing culture of inclusivity around those interests. For example, you might be a big Steelers fan, but your students may follow FC Barcelona (FC stands for Football or Fútbol Club, and it's a team that plays what most Americans call soccer). Just knowing a few of the top fútbol leagues and players will allow you to celebrate diversity from a point of view that is inclusive of sports played around the world.

Getting to know your students gets you access to all kinds of information about cultures *and* information that allows you to build better relationships with each individual student. Remember, at the center of minimizing bias to create more inclusive classrooms is relationship building with each individual student, because better relationships change students' lives and trajectories.

According to *Education Week* editor Sarah D. Sparks (2019):

> A Review of Educational Research analysis of 46 studies found that strong teacher-student relationships were associated in both the short- and long-term with improvements on practically every measure schools care about: higher student academic engagement, attendance, grades, fewer disruptive behaviors and suspensions, and lower school dropout rates.

Sparks (2019) additionally reports that good teacher-student relationships are also the best predictor of how much joy versus anxiety educators experience, so, win-win.

The more educators see diversity as a to-do list with checkboxes for Muslim, LGBTQ+, Black, Hispanic, Asian and Pacific Islander, Indigenous, female, differently abled people, and so on, the further away they get from celebrating true diversity. Celebrating true diversity is more than checking boxes on a to-do list. It should grow from a commitment to teaching truth and making sure that each student on your campus experiences a sense of belonging. Yes, there is bias in many systems and structures that needs to be addressed, and I believe that there is an element of activism in education. However, many times, that activism begins with doing your best for the one student standing right in front of you. When you build strong relationships with each of your students, you are already making a difference.

Ways to Celebrate Diversity Through Individuality

There is a saying in the Black community: "They're gonna take your Black card." While usually meant in jest, the thought that there are certain things that one has to do, think, say, and have to be considered Black is ludicrous (unless that thing is melanin). Cultural groups are not monolithic. Some groups practice culturally related traditions while some do not. Not all Black people listen to R&B, hip-hop, gospel, jazz, or blues, even though those are traditionally Black music genres. Conversely, not all people who listen to those genres are Black.

To disrupt the tendency to label and categorize people in your classroom and in your school, try using "all about me" activities on the first day to create interest groups in your class, in your grade level, or better yet, throughout your campus. When students identify interests and hobbies, color code them using markers, stick-on dots, or crayons, and hang them on the bulletin board. If everyone uses the same colors, you could regularly implement fun Fridays in which the skaters, the TikTokers, the coders, the readers, and so on get to meet and hang out. What better way to disrupt the segregation that still reigns in school lunchrooms? These groups need not be strictly bound by classroom, age, grade level, or cultural group—just their shared interests. Groups built around skater or coder culture will give students a chance to relate to each other according to interests rather than by age, melanin level, language, or gender identity. Figure 7.2 provides a step-by-step plan for how to celebrate diversity one student at a time, and figure 7.3 (page 104) is a sample set of questions that you could add to a Google Form as an "about me" survey.

Within this system, you may have a student alliance geared toward advocacy and support for marginalized groups. For example, on many college campuses there are student alliances or affinity groups designed to support populations that might otherwise not find support through mainstream school systems. These groups in secondary schools can be an important outlet and should be supported by the educators there. But the main goal here should be for students also to find commonality based on interests and hobbies. Not only do students (and teachers) form bonds based on shared interests but they have the opportunity to learn empathy and respect for others through a system unattached to the usual bias-provoking pathways, like gathering in the cafeteria along racial and gender fault lines.

According to Harvard Graduate School of Education's Making Caring Common Project (2018), empathy "requires practice and guidance." Sustained consideration of the perspectives and circumstances of others "helps make empathy a natural reflex and, through trial and error, helps children get better at tuning in to others' feelings

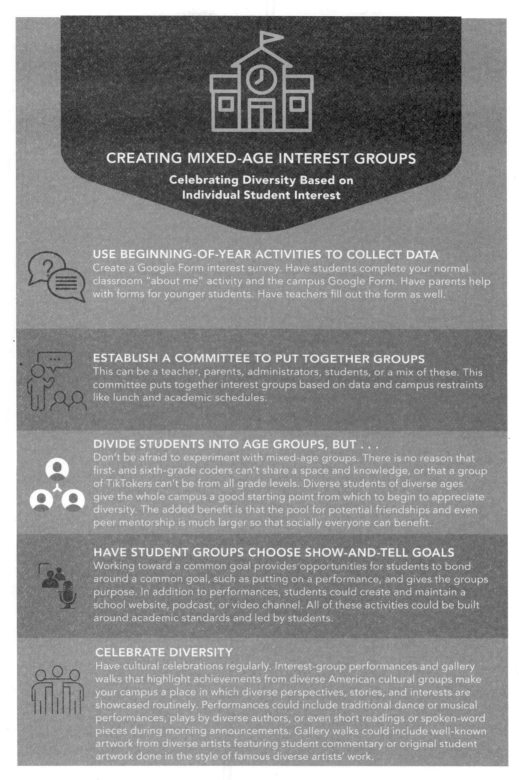

CREATING MIXED-AGE INTEREST GROUPS

Celebrating Diversity Based on Individual Student Interest

USE BEGINNING-OF-YEAR ACTIVITIES TO COLLECT DATA
Create a Google Form interest survey. Have students complete your normal classroom "about me" activity and the campus Google Form. Have parents help with forms for younger students. Have teachers fill out the form as well.

ESTABLISH A COMMITTEE TO PUT TOGETHER GROUPS
This can be a teacher, parents, administrators, students, or a mix of these. This committee puts together interest groups based on data and campus restraints like lunch and academic schedules.

DIVIDE STUDENTS INTO AGE GROUPS, BUT . . .
Don't be afraid to experiment with mixed-age groups. There is no reason that first- and sixth-grade coders can't share a space and knowledge, or that a group of TikTokers can't be from all grade levels. Diverse students of diverse ages give the whole campus a good starting point from which to begin to appreciate diversity. The added benefit is that the pool for potential friendships and even peer mentorship is much larger so that socially everyone can benefit.

HAVE STUDENT GROUPS CHOOSE SHOW-AND-TELL GOALS
Working toward a common goal provides opportunities for students to bond around a common goal, such as putting on a performance, and gives the groups purpose. In addition to performances, students could create and maintain a school website, podcast, or video channel. All of these activities could be built around academic standards and led by students.

CELEBRATE DIVERSITY
Have cultural celebrations regularly. Interest-group performances and gallery walks that highlight achievements from diverse American cultural groups make your campus a place in which diverse perspectives, stories, and interests are showcased routinely. Performances could include traditional dance or musical performances, plays by diverse authors, or even short readings or spoken-word pieces during morning announcements. Gallery walks could include well-known artwork from diverse artists featuring student commentary or original student artwork done in the style of famous diverse artists' work.

Figure 7.2: Creating mixed-age interest groups.

About Me

Let's get to know each other better. This is the place to tell me all about yourself!

Name

The name you like to be called

Class

How many siblings do you have?

What is your favorite thing to do outside of school?

What is your favorite music, song, or band?

Who is your favorite character or content creator and why? (Think cartoon, YouTuber, book, movie or series, and so on.)

What is your favorite food?

What is one fun fact about you?

What is your favorite school subject and why?

What is your least favorite school subject and why?

Do you have a pet? If so, tell me about it.

Do you have reliable internet at home?

- ○ Yes
- ○ No
- ○ Part of the time

Do you have any food allergies or other health concerns that I should know about?

If you could be in a group at school, what kind of group would it be?
- ○ Book
- ○ Movie
- ○ Singing
- ○ Dance
- ○ Coding
- ○ Band
- ○ Choir
- ○ Soccer
- ○ Basketball
- ○ Step
- ○ TikTok
- ○ Cooking
- ○ Board games
- ○ Other

Figure 7.3: Sample Google Form "about me" survey.

and perspectives" (Making Caring Common Project, 2018). By confronting bias, exploring diverse stories and perspectives, and examining culture in a broader sense, educators can help their students develop empathy and decrease instances of toxic othering and bullying.

Practicing Debate and Civil Disagreement

Teaching students that disagreeing on some things doesn't make you enemies is not only a way to honor diversity in the classroom; it's also good for society. Diversity and peace education expert Marisa Fasciano (2015) notes:

> Rather than asking your students to respect all belief systems, ask them to practice respecting all *people*, regardless of their belief system. Students don't need to agree with their classmates' religious or nonreligious beliefs, but they should be expected to interact with them in ways that are constructive and civil.

Integrating civil discourse and debate can be enriching in every content area. According to Harvard Graduate School of Education's Danxi Shen (n.d.), in a research review for Harvard's ABLConnect program, "Debating has been shown to facilitate engagement" and "is also found to improve learning outcomes." Practicing low-stakes conflict allows students to build relationships and practice the skills needed to show respect and empathy during more significant disagreements. Students can learn empathy for peers who prefer chocolate over vanilla ice cream, physics over biology, or science fair projects over basketball. Having students research and side against their own preferences gives students an additional opportunity to further learn about "others." Figure 7.4 (page 106) provides content-related themes for civil discussion and debate.

I don't explicitly mention social studies in this chart because so much of the content already lends itself to civic discourse. The list is also geared generally to grade 3 and above, but even the youngest students can discuss whether orange juice or apple juice is better and learn that the kind they don't prefer is not "gross" and that their best friend can still be their best friend if they don't like the same kind of juice. The point is to teach respect and empathy for people who make choices that might be different from their own. Empathy and respect are foundational to celebrating diversity.

Bring the World to Your Students

If the COVID-19 pandemic taught educators one thing, it's that they don't have to go somewhere to go somewhere. YouTube's augmented reality and virtual reality

Content or Subject	Discussion Themes	Cultural Context Connection
The arts	• Which epoch, genre, or artist is better? • Which instrument is best for solos? • What types of paints are better for ____? • Would Shakespeare be just as great if he were less well known? • What color is skin color or "flesh tone"?	• Each epoch, genre, or artist has strengths. • Many instruments can be used for solos; likewise the talents from diverse people and cultures can be highlighted. • While some types of paints are better for canvas, personal preference also plays a role. • He would. Likewise, there may be many other great playwrights who are not well known in the context of Western classical education. • "Nude," "beige," and "flesh" are all non-inclusive flesh tones. Crayola has developed sets of multishade skin-color crayons and markers useful for classrooms, perhaps especially low-diversity ones. Allowing young students to experience the full human flesh-tone spectrum affords them an opportunity to realize how diverse humans are early on.
Mathematics	• Where did mathematics come from? • Is it good or bad to use calculators? • Are people who are good at mathematics smart?	• Mathematics came out of the processes and thought schools of many different cultures like China (the abacus), Persia (algebra), Babylon (base 60 system), and Egypt (word problems), before Greek ones. • Many questions have more than one solution. • There are many kinds of ways to be smart; mathematics is only one.
Science	• Which branch of science is most important? • Should there be more people like Bill Nye on TV? • Were or are there women scientists?	• Each branch is important in teaching about the order of the world around us. • People who make science interesting and accessible can take learning into areas where there would otherwise be none, including remote areas. • While many resources highlight White, male scientists, good scientists come from all cultures and genders.

Content or Subject	Discussion Themes	Cultural Context Connection
English language arts	• Which is better, the British English spelling of words or the American spellings (grey or gray; favour or favor; and so on)? • Do audiobooks help or hinder people learning to read? • Should all students learn to read and write cursive?	• Sometimes we come to different versions of the same conclusions. • This question doesn't have a clear, correct answer—many questions do not. • Sometimes there are good arguments on both sides of an issue.
World languages	• English is one of the most commonly spoken languages in the world. Why do you think that is? • Mandarin and Hindi are the second and third most commonly spoken languages in the world. Why do you think more schools don't offer them? • What are the ten most spoken languages around the world?	• What part did colonization play in this development? • Is the Western classical education system biased against Eastern languages and cultures? • Why is English so popular even though it isn't the most commonly spoken language?
General	• Which is better: YouTube, Instagram, or TikTok? • Should school days be shortened? • Should education be free through college?	• Some personal preferences may have little to do with facts confirming that one thing is better than another. • Sometimes there are good arguments on both sides of an issue. Discuss and debate a few of them. • Economics and access play a part in a person's success and life trajectory. Not all students have equal access.

Figure 7.4: Themes for civil discussion and debate.

videos are legendary, and with some virtual reality goggles costing as little as six dollars, students can see museums, mountains, and mandolins virtually in situ. Additionally, students can learn to write in Mandarin or spell in American Sign Language, learn traditional Cree or Choctaw dances, watch foreign films, and view student performances and projects from all over the world via various virtual and social media outlets.

Additionally, if you use Spotify or any other online playlist, you can play music from any part of the world. Have students spin a globe to pick a place and play music from that region during any time you would regularly play music in class. Make sure your students know that "I don't like that" and "That's weird" are not respectful comments. Students can voice displeasure, but you can encourage them to respectfully critique the music (for example, "It's too loud," "The sound is scratchy," or "It's too high pitched"). Comments should be held until the music has played for a specified time to give students the opportunity to experience the sounds before voicing their opinions.

New and unfamiliar things often meet resistance. This is a perfect exercise to remind students of that. If something is wildly unpopular, you don't have to commit to listen for the whole time, but ask your students what positive attributes they can find in the music. If your class finds music they really like, share it with your colleagues on campus or through social media. Teachers are always looking for a good clean playlist, and this way, you and your class will be helping others to celebrate diversity as well. One final tip for using playlists: countries rarely have just one type of music. United States? Jazz, Tejano, and zydeco. France? Chanson and French hip-hop. Australia? Corroboree and Aussie rock. Korea? Pungmul and K-pop. Spinning the globe to explore diverse modern and traditional music through listening is one of the most enjoyable ways to celebrate diversity. It's also a way to introduce diverse narratives without being "controversial."

Content Mastery Through Culture

Learning through and about various cultures should not be an add-on. If students are doing research projects, multimedia projects, geography projects, book reports, project-based learning, or even STEM assignments, they can master content standards while increasing cultural literacy. Figure 7.5 provides ideas for possible projects and assignments for various subjects.

Other ways to make culture and diversity part of your daily routine are to add cultural facts to morning announcements, construct and post a cultural inclusion

Project	Brief Description	Content Connections
Recipe Book	Students collect recipes from friends, family, or the internet. Recipes may not be for "American" fare but should be connected to students' own heritage (German grandma's knödel, Ethiopian injera, or Italian great-grandpa's gelato, for example).	Technology: recipe book layout and graphics Mathematics: recipe measurements and conversions from metric to U.S. customary units Social studies: culture, language, clothing, geography, terrain, and climate English language arts: storytelling and histories like where the recipe came from, where the relatives came from, and how those people came to America Health and physical education: nutrition
Family History Oral or Written Reports	Students use the internet or family interviews to collect as much information as they can on their families going back as far as possible.	Mathematics: pictographs or charts using heads to denote generations. Students can have a column or a separate pictograph depicting how many generations they went back. Older students can make family trees or organigrams. Social studies: culture, geography, and history English language arts: storytelling and histories Social-emotional learning: building connections with family and relatives
Campus Fun Fact Statistic Charts: *Everyone's From Somewhere*	Using peer and teacher interviews, find out interesting facts, like where classmates' and teachers' families came from, what languages they spoke or speak, what foods come from those regions, what sports are played, what music is made, and so on. Display them all and see who's related (who has Irish roots, whose family lived in Louisiana, and so on).	Technology: creating a Google Form with interview questions Social studies: culture, geography, and history English language arts: storytelling and histories Mathematics: graphs and charts Social-emotional learning: building connections with peers and teachers Physical education: students can play variations of four square or other games using the knowledge they gather from interviews. For example, student one has a ball and starts by saying, "I grew up in California." Student two signals for the ball, student one throws it, and student two responds on catching it, "My mom is from California, but she grew up in Louisiana." Student three signals and catches the ball, saying, "My sister goes to college in Louisiana, but she's getting married to someone from New York." The game continues with students making new connections with each previous student whenever they catch the ball.

continued →

Figure 7.5: Teaching through culture.

Project	Brief Description	Content Connections
TV Series or Movie Reviews	Have secondary students watch popular movie clips or series episodes featuring a cultural group other than their own and write reviews based on how accurately they perceive the other culture is portrayed. The review should include research and honest but respectful discourse about stereotypes, clichéd portrayals, and the harm these can cause. For example, a student might review *The Karate Kid* and address the portrayal of Mr. Miyagi with his very strong accent. This can be done individually or in small groups.	English language arts: nonfiction writing conventions. Reviews should be well written, with few grammatical, punctuation, and usage errors. Social studies: culture, stereotypes Social-emotional learning: reflecting on bias Technology: formatting and layout of the review. Encourage students to add graphics or even memes where appropriate.
Writing Prompt: What does it feel like to be _____?	Have students write about what it feels like to be themselves: female, White, Cree, gender fluid, male, autistic, athletic, and so on. Have them describe what they feel their position is in the world based on how they identify. Alternately, have them write about what it would feel like to be born someone else. If there is time, have them combine the two and write about whether they would be better or worse off as someone other than who they are.	English language arts: nonfiction writing conventions Social studies: culture, stereotypes Social-emotional learning: reflecting on bias and privilege Technology: formatting and layout of the essay. Encourage students to add graphics or images.

mission statement next to your class rules, hold a cultural potluck featuring foods from diverse cultures, or even connect with schools in other communities, regions, or countries. A class mission statement could be a short, two- to four-sentence pledge or commitment to making your area of the school a welcoming space for all. And if you are interested in connecting with other educators, Twitter is a space where educators meet and connect. Some hashtags to look for are #education, #teacher, and #edchat. Content hashtags like #ela, #mathchat, and #finearts can offer good starting points as well.

The point is, if you want the needle to move on diversity and inclusion, you need to make sure that you don't treat celebrating diversity like a fancy outfit that gets taken out from its place in the back of the closet once a year. Celebrating diversity should be a part of your everyday experience and a part of the daily learning experiences you design for your students.

Reflection to Action

You've come again to the time when your reflection and journaling will take center stage. When you finish your notes and personal chapter reflection, thoughtfully answer the following questions.

1. How can you get your peers to recognize diversity as more than Black, White, brown, and so on?

2. What kinds of lessons do you already use that you can add a cultural component to?

3. Why is celebrating diversity important in schools with low-diversity populations?

4. How have events since the death of George Floyd in 2020 shown a need for more explicit instruction on diversity, empathy, and civil discourse?

Once you have completed the questions, choose one activity from table 7.1 (page 112) to try this week.

Table 7.1: Sharing What I've Learned About Ensuring Representation Throughout the Year, Not Just During "Months"

Group	Activity
Littles (preK–grade 3)	Showcase cultures by doing artwork and decorating for diverse holidays like Diwali, Chinese New Year, Ramadan, Hanukkah, and others. Keep books on diverse cultures with the other books rather than moving them to a special section, making sure that there is a good selection of fiction as well as nonfiction.
Middles (grades 4–7)	Find a class in another part of the world to collaborate with. Twitter is a great way to meet educators from all over the world. Share a celebration, have pen pals, or play a Mystery Skype-type game in which students ask each other questions to figure out the location of the other class. This can be done synchronously or asynchronously.
Secondary	Have students put together a digital "one hundred days of diversity" calendar with pictures, short videos, minibios, and other fun facts about diverse people, cultures, and celebrations. Have students google "famous [insert cultural group here] [insert role here: musician, scientist, pilot, and so on]." One easily accessible way to complete this project is to have students decorate slides and add them all to a shared portfolio. Other ways include using Book Creator (https://bookcreator.com), Canva (www.canva.com), or even a collection of TikTok-styled clips.
Staff	Use the resources from the student calendar in the previous row to decorate hallways and boards, or add items to the school announcements. Educators can also use the resources to integrate the achievements of diverse people into classroom lessons.
Parents and Community	Share the calendar with the community as a digital download for students of all ages. Consider reaching out to the surrounding community to have speakers come in and do short talks about the facts and celebrations found in the calendar.

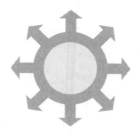

CHAPTER EIGHT

Bias in Action: Avoid Missteps

I still remember my first trip abroad at age twenty. I was walking through the streets of Palermo, Italy, when a man, along with his wife and child, came up to me exclaiming, "*Bella, bella*!"—pretty, pretty. They touched my hair and my face, and I remember soaking in their reverence at what I guessed was my uncommon brown face and curly hair. I remember feeling alarmed but also like some exotic princess. A few years later in Israel, a man told me I was beautiful and that I was what was called *délicatesse*, which is French for tasty or dainty. It made my skin crawl. I didn't feel like an exotic princess—I felt reduced, objectified.

Although I would consider neither of these exchanges racist or mean-spirited, they reflect a kind of derogatory behavior that falls under the category of a microaggression. Oxford University Press defines *microaggression* (n.d.) as "indirect, subtle, or unintentional discrimination against members of a marginalized group." The eighth and final guiding principle focuses on these harmful words and actions: avoid microaggressions (see figure 8.1, page 114).

Being touched about the head is an invasion of personal space, and being called a delicacy is only complimentary if you're on a shelf in the fine food section of a store. Counseling psychology scholar Derald Wing Sue (2010) explains that microaggressions come in three forms.

- **Microassaults:** Actions that are conscious and intentionally discriminatory

- **Microinsults:** Communications relaying rudeness and insensitivity that demean another's racial heritage or identity; these can be verbal, nonverbal, or environmental

- **Microinvalidations:** More subtle communications that exclude, negate, or nullify the thoughts, feelings, or experiential reality of a person of color

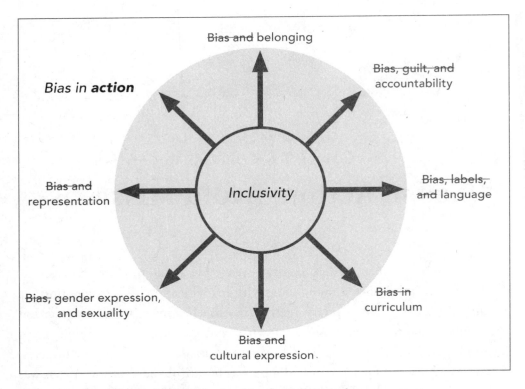

Figure 8.1: Guiding principle 8—Avoid microaggressions.

I will in good faith assume that microassaults, like using racial slurs or posting swastikas and race- or gender-based slurs to social media, are things you recognize as wrong, so this chapter will wade through the finer points of microinsults and microinvalidations.

Microinsults: Please, Don't Do This

Let's start with hair touching. It seems that Black people have finally come out of the closet about hair touching, because if you do an online search for "touching Black people's hair," you will find a few pages of results. I can't tell you the first time someone asked to touch my hair. Someone at school was always asking about my hair, asking to touch it, or just touching it without asking. Hair touching not only reduces people to exotic curiosities but also makes them anxious. Journalist and author Allison Keyes (2010) does a good job of examining the phenomenon in equal parts humor and earnestness, and her message is clear: "What you ought to do, is keep your hands outta my hair, unless I invite you to touch it."

Exploring Your Mind's (2018) psychology article tells us that "people need safe, personal space to feel protected, reduce stress, and remain focused." That is what students—and teachers—need to learn, and it's an easy fix. No unwarranted touching. Other things on the no-no list include the following.

- Asking Muslim girls to show you their hair or remove their hijab (or allowing students to do so)

- Assuming gender norms; for example, sending boys to the trucks or girls away from them

- Wearing any cultural clothing for Halloween, including but not limited to sombreros, feathered headdresses or Indigenous costumes, Day of the Dead makeup, bindis, or turbans; hopefully, it goes without saying that you should avoid blackface, braid wigs, or afros unless it's *Madagascar* zebra "Afro Circus" themed

These and other no-nos may seem small and insignificant, but over the course of a lifetime, they cause physical and mental changes that mirror trauma responses. Microaggression trauma is:

> the excessive and continuous exposure to subtle discrimination (both interpersonal and systemic) and the subsequent symptoms that develop or persist as a result. Although not all microaggressions are life threatening, they can certainly be pervasive and compromise one's sense of psychological and emotional safety, resulting in typical symptoms associated with trauma. (Nadal, 2018, p. 13)

This kind of trauma is real, and it is a part of daily life for far too many people. Being colorblind is not the answer. In fact, individuals *want* to be seen, heard, and accepted. So pay attention to these differences and celebrate them in a way that lets students know you appreciate them. For instance, just because hair touching is a no-no doesn't mean that hair complimenting is. If new braids, haircuts, and hair colors show up in class, students should know that you notice. You just don't want to focus *only* on what makes a person different. If you fixate on some aspect of a student's difference, you are likely to react to that difference, like asking your Mexican student what she's doing for Hispanic Heritage Month instead of asking all your students what they are planning for Hispanic Heritage Month. And, when you pay more attention to the ways you are similar, you are more likely to avoid snafus involving racial, cultural, or sexual identity.

Microinsults can be difficult to recognize and mitigate. People often put other people into categories without realizing it. Have you heard, thought, or even said any of the following? "Wow, you're so tall; you play basketball, right?" Or, "Science fair? You look like a cheerleader." On the surface, either of those statements may seem complimentary or could be accurate. But assuming that all tall boys are interested in basketball or that pretty, popular girls can't be interested in science or even that all cheerleaders have to be a certain "type" is problematic. The trick here is to ask more than you assume and listen more than you talk. You can never go wrong with asking instead of categorizing when you have only superficial information. Instead of making assumptions based on personal biases or stereotypes, ask your students what hobbies they have, what they are interested in, and if they are in any clubs or organizations.

Taking ownership of the way you act on hidden biases or blind spots can help you implement action steps and modify your behavior to ensure that you don't throw stumbling blocks onto the paths of your most vulnerable learners. Some unintentionally biased questions and statements appear in figures 3.5 and 3.6 (page 39). I cover additional microaggressions and microinsults in figure 8.2.

Sometimes, it's not implicit bias or categorizing; sometimes, it's just repeating things we hear without thinking of the implication. Consider the phrases *Indian giver* and *Indian summer*. Both have racist undertones, conveying a derogatory lack of understanding for Indigenous culture. *Jewing someone down* or *gypping* someone at a flea market are still in common usage, but both carry negative stereotypes for Jewish and Romani people. There are many more examples of common phrases with racist or misogynistic backgrounds, like *mumbo jumbo, sold down the river, rule of thumb,* or even *long time no see,* but the idea is not to police speech, only to cause you to consider whether or not you marginalize people with your word choices. Should you want to learn more, a google search of *racist and sexist origins of common phrases* will yield results. Babbel Magazine offers a resource at www.babbel.com/en/magazine /common-racist-words-phrases that offers a good starting point.

Microinvalidations: We're All the Same, Right?

Another way to show bias is to assume that your experience is universal. Assuming that everyone has the same chance to succeed is a microinvalidation that ignores the hurdles historically and currently set for some populations. Telling students that they just need to work harder to be successful is one way of invalidating the experiences of marginalized populations. This is especially true in students under the special

How to Stay Away From Unintentional Slights and Microaggressions

What a handsome young man; I bet you're real popular with the girls on campus!

Don't assume that the student considers being popular with the girls complimentary. Also, this compliments something that a student cannot work to attain.

You're on the _____ team? Congratulations! That took focus and hard work!

Compliment a student's work ethic and other attributes within the student's locus of control.

You are so inspiring!

Whether students have a difficult home situation, come from another country, or are differently abled, this statement says that you have low expectations for them.

Good work on _____.

Compliments should be specific and based on students' personal efforts, not their efforts in comparison with other students who are completing the same tasks (and not being called inspiring).

Will your husband be joining us? or Is this your sister?

Families come in all forms. A student's village can be made of many different constellations. Assuming relationships can make for unnecessarily awkward moments. Assuming relationships and pronouns can also convey a bias against the evolving and varied structures of families.

Hi, I'm Ms. Nichols!

Let the adults in your students' lives introduce themselves, providing as much or as little information as they care to. If an adult is showing up for your student, assume this person is a supportive part of a student's circle.

Note: This content also appears on https://hedreich.com/blog in a slightly different form.

Figure 8.2: Avoiding microinsults—Positive and negative comments.

education umbrella who have invisible challenges. While no one would assume that a student in a wheelchair could run a marathon by trying harder, it's not uncommon for teachers to consider students with ADHD lazy or unmotivated. Students who are neurodivergent in some invisible way suffer that kind of bias often. Clinical mental health professional Lynn Fraley (n.d.) asserts, "There are way too many people who fall through the cracks and are expected to accomplish tasks that are outside their current abilities simply because caregivers, family members, educators and doctors fail to recognize their challenges." Assuming that a student can do something because you could is another type of microinvalidation.

A further example of microinvalidation is the kind you can find in places where there is a general lack of female or BIPOC representation. Students of color in private schools, for example, often hear things like "I guess you're on scholarship" or "Lucky for you this school has an affirmative action program." These statements assume that a student of color, one who is differently abled, or one who is in some other way different could not have earned a spot in a prestigious learning institution. The thoughts undergirding statements like these stem from the erroneous belief that either everyone can succeed if they work hard enough or BIPOCs, women, or differently abled people get an unfair advantage because of government programs like affirmative action. The problem with either of those assumptions is that they ignore the uneven playing field cultivated through generations of systemic disenfranchisement. Remember, for example, Black people in the United States could not legally vote until the passing of the Fifteenth Amendment, and even then it was only in theory. Women could not vote until the passing of the Nineteenth Amendment in 1920; in other places, this right was won even more recently, such as Switzerland in 1991 and Saudi Arabia in 2015 (Aspinall, 2021; Krulwich, 2016). Many countries, including the United States, face barriers like restrictive voting laws, gerrymandering, and voter intimidation (Aspinall, 2021). To further bring home the point that even the big civil rights issues are not yet behind us, the oldest school segregation case in Louisiana was settled in 2016 (Thomas, 2018). The Freedom for All Americans litigation tracker (https://freedomforallamericans.org/litigation-tracker) can provide insight and information on the kinds of civil rights cases that are currently ongoing. The point is that marginalized groups have historically faced numerous barriers, and microinvalidations brush these well-documented issues aside.

Microassaults are overt forms of racism and can also happen unintentionally. People telling racist or sexist jokes, store managers following people of color around a store, or customer service agents being dismissive of people with accents are all overtly offensive behaviors. While these kinds of behaviors happen less frequently when people are working on mitigating their biases, they do still happen.

Recurring, small acts of aggression make a big impact on the health and well-being of those who experience them. Whether as microinvalidations, microinsults, or microassaults, the societal outcomes continue to impact historically marginalized communities. Figure 8.3 documents some examples and outcomes of such statements and actions.

MICROAGGRESSIONS
MACRO IMPACT

Examples of microaggressions

Microinsult

Telling a student from the nondominant culture (with incredulity) that he is articulate; calling a South American colleague "spicy" when she expresses her opinion firmly

Microassault

Racial profiling; asking a Hispanic American to "show papers"; using the birth name (deadnaming) or incorrect pronouns for a transgender or nonbinary person

Microinvalidation

Telling a Black man that White people are also stopped by the police, but they comply, so there are no adverse outcomes; asking an Asian American where she's *really* from

Outcomes of microaggressions

Social

- Avoidance
- Fear
- Isolation
- Hypervigilance

Cognitive

- Self-doubt
- Depression
- Executive function difficulties
- Hopelessness

Physical

- Headaches
- Chronic exhaustion
- Self-harm
- Hypertension
- Insomnia

Figure 8.3: Examples and outcomes of microaggressions.

The next time you see a student in AP classes, chess club, the science fair, or another situation on campus that has traditionally been a space in which diverse populations are underrepresented, remember that your reactions may add to or detract from that student's social, academic, mental, and even physical well-being.

What Are You Thinking?

This is the section of the book that brings us back to the beginning, to bias, belonging, and the thoughts that undergird many of your daily, automatic actions. Are you recommending Angie Thomas's (2017) *The Hate U Give* to Jamal instead of Shakespeare's *Julius Caesar* because it's a really great book or because you think he'll be better served reading something closer to what you consider his lived experience to be? Did you ask José to play Selina's father in the school play because he's a strong actor or because you think he'll be able to do a really good Mexican accent? Sometimes, it's not what you do or say but your motivations that cause pain to students and peers, and constitute a microaggression. When I was in the sixth grade, I had a teacher who I was sure didn't like me, as I told my mother many times. When she asked why I thought that, I could only say that it was a feeling I had. Without more to go on, she gave my complaints very little credence until she met the teacher herself. I remember her saying that at the parent-teacher meeting, the teacher acknowledged that I was doing well academically but went on to complain about personality traits that she found "not serious enough" or "too bubbly." Needless to say, my mother finally understood what I had been trying to tell her all along; the teacher just didn't like me. Students are savvy, and they know what you think about them, even if you might think it's not obvious. Moreover, they *care* about what you think. As Sparks (2019) reminds us in chapter 7 (page 99), good relationships are fundamental to student success, and they affect academic and social-emotional outcomes both in the short and long term.

Building relationships is something that should be done with intentionality—so is weeding out implicit bias. Make time now to take inventory of your thoughts and feelings about your students. If you have time, do it for each student. If time is short, at least take this inventory for the students you have the strongest feelings about, whether positive or negative. For instance, if you have a student who always brings a smile to your face, one who reminds you of why you got into teaching, examine why you feel that way about her. Figure 8.4 is a tool for you to critically examine what you think about each of your students so that you can become more aware of the impact your thoughts have on students. Knowing your blind spots and biases in connection with the way they specifically affect your individual students will help you become more intentional in mitigating negative student outcomes.

What did you learn? What did you find out? Did you learn more about who you are likely to favor and why? Did you notice any patterns? Are there certain personalities that are more likely to rub you wrong? Do you have more work to do than you thought? Wherever you are in your journey, give yourself permission to be right

Student Name	Biased Thoughts	Potential Harm
Example: Thien Pham	Put her in AP-track mathematics. Asian students always excel in mathematics and science.	Thien may or may not be good at or even interested in mathematics or science. Additionally, there might be another student better suited to the AP track who might get overlooked because of the tendency to assume that all Asians are good in STEM courses.
Example: Meridyth Johnson	She has a history of office referrals; she'll probably be trouble.	Instead of building a relationship with this student and working toward a breakthrough, she's sent to the office the first time she says anything disagreeable because of her reputation with others.

Figure 8.4: My students, my biases.

*Visit **go.SolutionTree.com/diversityandequity** for a free reproducible version of this figure.*

where you are. Only transparency will allow you to be the inclusive teacher you're working toward being.

The information in this chapter has hopefully opened your eyes to the little ways that teachers can harm students daily, but in no way does it constitute a definitive list of what and what not to say and do. The most important thing you can do to build better relationships and support the better student outcomes that good relationships bring is to learn what kinds of interactions cause harm and avoid them. Beyond that, on the outside chance that students do let you know they've been offended, believe them and show empathy. So often, when others call attention to a slight, teachers brush their feelings off with phrases that fall far short of the intended de-escalation they might usually be going for; this constitutes a microinvalidation. Telling a student—or a peer—that a comment "wasn't meant that way" or "was not meant to be offensive" invalidates their feelings and causes further harm. As Michèle Lamont, researcher and director of Harvard's Weatherhead Center for International Affairs, puts it, "The everyday experience of African-Americans is one that is painful because they constantly experience stigmatization, being misunderstood, ignored, stereotyped as slow or poorly educated, even if they're middle class" (Powell, 2016). That holds true for other groups that have been marginalized as well. By the time people are courageous enough to respond honestly to a microaggression, chances are that they have experienced the same microinsult many times. Be the one to hear them, show empathy, and move to corrective action.

Reflection to Action

Take out your journal for this, the final guiding principle. While reading the pages of *Finding Your Blind Spots*, you have probably learned quite a bit about how to create more welcoming classroom and campus spaces for all your students. You've probably learned even more about yourself. Take this time to reflect and bring some sense of closure to this chapter of your learning. Then, consider writing down which chapters of the book you'd like to revisit first to deepen your knowledge. Again, be transparent. And if there are any student names you'd like to write in the margin as a reminder to give those relationships some extra attention, do that too.

1. In figure 8.4 (page 121), were you more aware or more surprised at your reflections and connections? If you were more aware, what factors contributed to that awareness? If you were more surprised, what do you need to change in order to be more aware of your biases?

2. Have you ever experienced microaggressions? How did you respond? How did it impact the relationship with the person who offended you?

3. What's one change you can make with one student tomorrow?

4. Name one educator you work with who would be open to learning about microaggressions and the other concepts you learned about in chapter 8. How can you approach and maybe even invite that person to be one of your accountability partners?

Now that you have reflected on what you've learned about the eighth guiding principle, you are ready to use what you've learned to make an impact (see table 8.1).

Table 8.1: Sharing What I've Learned About What Not to Do

Group	Activity
Littles (preK–grade 3)	Teach the Golden Rule: treat others as you would want to be treated. Asking young students how they would feel if _____ is a good way to help them develop empathy. For example: "How would you feel if someone said something mean to you about your favorite outfit?" or "What would you do if you heard someone use unkind words about your friend?"
	Talk about cultural diversity and the way people identify in respectful terms. For example: "Yes, Coach Lance has a husband, not a wife. Couples can be all kinds of combinations of people" or "Yes, David has very beautiful dark brown skin, just like you have very lovely rosy cheeks. Isn't it great how we can be the same and different all at once?" Reference figure 3.2 (page 35) when referring to diverse populations so that students learn respectful language.
Middles (grades 4–7)	Using figures 3.2 (page 35) and 3.4 (page 37), talk about how to refer to people respectfully. Discuss why people feel uncomfortable talking about race, culture, and gender, and establish norms for open and respectful discourse. Ask, "Why do you think . . .?" and "How do you feel when . . .?" and let the conversations evolve. Avoid guiding the conversation. The point is to allow student critical thinking and empathy to come to the forefront.
Secondary	Reviewing figure 3.2 (page 35), talk about social media behaviors and microaggressions. Have students provide examples of negative online interactions and then have a class discussion about why people belittle each other. Consider having students write a mission statement about how to make social media platforms a safe space for everybody. Discuss also how to use social media for good by asking students what kinds of positive things they've learned from it and what kinds of positive content they could create and share.
	Consider having students practice social activism by creating and posting video clips explaining the importance of labels and using the terms in figure 3.2. Post them on your class social media page.
Staff	Review figures 3.2 (page 35) and 3.4 (page 37). Make sure that teachers, administrators, and staff know how to refer to diverse populations correctly.
	If you don't have one already, have students create a statement in support of your campus as a safe space for all. This goes beyond condemning bullying. Make it a priority to make your campus a place where all students and staff members are welcomed and included.
Parents and Community	Share the mission statement your class created with your families and communities through newsletters, social media, and your class web page. If there is pushback about a "liberal agenda," cite bullying, hate crimes, youth suicide rates, and your desire to protect and include all students and perspectives. Ensure that parents and the community know that your campus will not tolerate people being made to feel small for any reason.

Conclusion

In conclusion, there is no conclusion. The most important thought I want to leave you with is that inclusivity is not a one-and-done kind of thing. Being a reflective practitioner is like clean eating. Either it's a lifestyle or the changes won't stick.

What have you learned that stands out most? Was it something about how you relate to others in your family? What about how you relate to students who are most unlike you? Maybe you did not find the most impactful learning in this book; maybe you found it within yourself.

What are your big takeaways about how you other? What have been your most shocking self-discoveries? Which of those discoveries have you tackled, and which of your thought processes and patterns will you leave for another time? These are the questions that will guide you further on your journey. *Finding Your Blind Spots* is a book you can revisit again and again. Remember figure 5.3 (page 72), in which you could pick a familial relationship to invest in? Well, if you only have one relative that you could stand to have a closer relationship with, count yourself lucky. Many people avoid family gatherings—even when the world isn't besieged by a pandemic. Pick a second relative, or better yet, do a chapter study with your family! And how about practicing to respectfully disagree with those who espouse different ideologies? Are your social media posts a reflection of a kind and empathetic person, even when you're triggered? Is your classroom a safe space for civil discourse and respectful disagreement? Teaching ground rules for civil disagreement is something, unfortunately, that many educators have left out of their classrooms. Teachers might say, "Use your nice words" or "Be respectful," but there are real lessons that humanize the "other side," which I have included in the pages of this book. Why are racism, sexism, ableism, and other types of discrimination bad? Because words and deeds that stem from them hurt people, often people who have been already hurt repeatedly. In chapter 7 (page 99), I told you that many times, activism is about doing your best for the one student standing right in front of you. If you begin to talk less about the buzzwords associated with social justice and more about character, empathy, and human kindness, you can begin to see your interactions as a reflection of who you want to be.

When you think about the kind of teacher—or person—you want to be, focus on one of your triggers, one that you really believe is justified. Ask yourself how holding on to that belief or notion will impact your relationships with your students. How can demonizing little Jimmy's mom because she's left-wing, right-wing, Christian, gay, Muslim, Black, Jewish, White, just plain wrong, or any other label you can think of help build a better world? How will it help prevent schoolyard squabbles or make your classroom a safe space for a student who desperately needs one? When you begin to put the emphasis on character rather than on labels or categories, you begin to relate differently to others, even those whose motivations or ideals you may not understand.

Even with all the reflections and questions presented in this book, there is still one very important question you should ask yourself: What's your why? It can't be the money or the status, and it certainly isn't for the summers off that never quite materialize. If you chose this profession because you want to be *that* educator that students remember when they get their engineering degree or when they teach their own children numbers and letters, then this is your moment. The only person getting in your way of changing the world one student at a time is you.

Finding Your Blind Spots is, on the surface, a book about mitigating bias and creating more equity in the classroom. While it is that, it goes beyond that scope to be about good teaching and about social-emotional learning and the well-being of your students—all of your students. *Finding Your Blind Spots* is about making space inside yourself to have empathy for each of your students—the ones most like you and the ones most unlike you. It's a book that starts with you looking inward, a book that keeps you coming back to that bench where you "set a spell" with just yourself. Only you know if your ideologies are more important to you than being the best educator you can be for each student whose life you touch. But my guess is, if you are here, you're destined to be one of the good ones.

Keep learning, keep reflecting, keep cycling back through the eight guiding principles for overcoming implicit bias and creating more inclusive classrooms and campuses. I'll be rooting for you.

References and Resources

Adler, M., & Harper, L. M. (2018). Race and ethnicity in classification systems: Teaching knowledge organization from a social justice perspective. *Library Trends, 67*(1), 52–73.

Albert, N. (2016). *Embracing love: My journey to hugging a man in his underwear.* Canton, MI: Read the Spirit Books.

American Academy of Child and Adolescent Psychiatry. (2019). *Lesbian, gay, bisexual and transgender parents.* Accessed at www.aacap.org/AACAP/Families_and_Youth/Facts _for_Families/FFF-Guide/Children-with-Lesbian-Gay-Bisexual-and-Transgender -Parents-092.aspx on May 10, 2021.

American Association of University Women. (n.d.). *Early gender bias.* Accessed at www .aauw.org/issues/education/gender-bias on May 10, 2021.

American Psychological Association. (2018). *A glossary: Defining transgender terms.* Accessed at www.apa.org/monitor/2018/09/ce-corner-glossary on May 10, 2021.

American Psychological Association Style. (2019). *Bias-free language.* Accessed at https:// apastyle.apa.org/style-grammar-guidelines/bias-free-language on May 10, 2021.

Annamma, S. A., Anyon, Y., Joseph, N. M., Farrar, J., Greer, E., Downing, B., et al. (2019). Black girls and school discipline: The complexities of being overrepresented and understudied. *Urban Education, 54*(2), 211–242. Accessed at https://doi .org/10.1177/0042085916646610 on May 10, 2021.

Appel, M., & Kronberger, N. (2012). Stereotypes and the achievement gap: Stereotype threat prior to test taking. *Educational Psychology Review, 24*(4), 609–635. Accessed at www.jstor.org/stable/43546808 on September 1, 2021.

Arefin, D. S. (2020). *Is hair discrimination race discrimination?* Accessed at www .americanbar.org/groups/business_law/publications/blt/2020/05/hair-discrimination on May 10, 2021.

Aspinall, G. (2021, August 3). *Here are the countries where it's still really difficult for women to vote.* Accessed at https://graziadaily.co.uk/life/real-life/countries-where-women-can -t-vote/ on September 13, 2021.

Balvin, N. (2017, August 18). *What is gender socialization and why does it matter?* Accessed at https://blogs.unicef.org/evidence-for-action/what-is-gender-socialization-and-why-does-it-matter/#:~:text=Gender%20socialization%20begins%20at%20birth,the%20UNICEF%20Office%20of%20Research%20%E2%80%93 on May 10, 2021.

Baskin, C. (2002). Circles of resistance: Spirituality in social work practice, education and transformative change. *Currents: New Scholarship in the Human Services, 1*(1), 2–9.

Baysu, G., & Phalet, K. (2019). The up- and downside of dual identity: Stereotype threat and minority performance. *Journal of Social Issues, 75*(2), 568–591. Accessed at https://doi.org/10.1111/josi.12330 on May 10, 2021.

Berlin, I. (2013). *Three critics of the Enlightenment: Vico, Hamann, Herder* (2nd ed.). Princeton, NJ: Princeton University Press.

Beukeboom, C. J., & Burgers, C. (2019). How stereotypes are shared through language: A review and introduction of the social categories and stereotypes communication (SCSC) framework. *Review of Communication Research, 7*, 1–37. Accessed at https://doi.org/10.12840/issn.2255-4165.017 on May 10, 2021.

Biola Magazine Staff. (2015, December 31). *How should Christians respond to gay friends or family members?* Accessed at www.biola.edu/blogs/biola-magazine/2015/how-should-christians-respond-to-gay-friends-or-fa on September 10, 2021.

Birner, B. (Ed.). (n.d.). *Is English changing?* Accessed at www.linguisticsociety.org/content/english-changing on May 10, 2021.

Blackstock, C. (2011). The emergence of the breath of life theory. *Journal of Social Work Values and Ethics, 8*(1), 1–16.

Bloom, B. S. (Ed.). (1956). *Taxonomy of educational objectives: The classification of educational goals; Handbook I: Cognitive domain.* New York: McKay.

Bridging Divides Initiative. (2021, February). *Report: Election 2020 political violence data and trends.* Accessed at https://bridgingdivides.princeton.edu/news/2021/report-election-2020-political-violence-data-and-trends on September 14, 2021.

Broonzy, W. L. C. (2000). Black, brown and white. On *Trouble in Mind* [Vinyl record]. Washington, DC: Smithsonian Folkways. (January 1952)

Brown, J., & Ellis, A. (1968). Say it loud—I'm Black and I'm proud [Recorded by J. Brown]. On *Say It Loud—I'm Black and I'm Proud* [Vinyl single]. Cincinnati, OH: King Records. (August 7, 1968)

Bunker, L. (2017). *Felix Yz.* New York: Viking.

Burton, N. (2020). *Heaven and hell: The psychology of the emotions* (2nd ed.). Oxford, UK: Acheron Press.

Centers for Disease Control and Prevention. (n.d.). *About underlying cause of death, 1999–2019.* Accessed at https://wonder.cdc.gov/ucd-icd10.html on May 11, 2021.

Cheryan, S., & Bodenhausen, G. V. (2000). When positive stereotypes threaten intellectual performance: The psychological hazards of "model minority" status.

Psychological Science, 11(5), 399–402. Accessed at https://doi.org/10.1111/1467 -9280.00277 on May 10, 2021.

Classical. (n.d.). In *Merriam-Webster's online dictionary.* Accessed at www.merriam-webster.com/dictionary/classical on June 10, 2021.

Colorín Colorado. (n.d.). *What are BICS and CALP?* Accessed at www.colorincolorado .org/faq/what-are-bics-and-calp on September 9, 2021.

Coming out. (n.d.). In *Open Education Sociology Dictionary.* Accessed at https:// sociologydictionary.org/coming-out on May 10, 2021.

The Conscious Kid. (2020, June 18). *Do you remember any of these from when you were a kid? Have you heard any of them recently with* [Photographs]. Instagram. Accessed at www.instagram.com/p/CBl1hGfJ95h/?igshid=1w5ct7lk2yczl on June 10, 2021.

Cooper, T. (2019). Calling out 'alternative facts': Curriculum to develop students' capacity to engage critically with contradictory sources. *Teaching in Higher Education, 24*(3), 444–459. Accessed at https://doi.org/10.1080/13562517.2019.1566220 on May 10, 2021.

Copeland, L. (2018, April). *When guilt is good.* Accessed at www.theatlantic.com /magazine/archive/2018/04/how-to-guilt-trip-your-kids/554102/ on June 9, 2021.

Coqual. (2019). *Being black in corporate America: An intersectional exploration.* Accessed at www.talentinnovation.org/publication.cfm?publication=1650 on May 10, 2021.

Create a Respectful and Open Workplace for Natural Hair Act, 58 California Code, § 212.1, 12926 (2019).

Croizet, J., & Claire, T. (1998). Extending the concept of stereotype threat to social class: The intellectual underperformance of students from low socioeconomic backgrounds. *Personality and Social Psychology Bulletin, 24*(6), 588–594.

Cropanzano, R. S., Massaro, S., & Becker, W. J. (2017). Deontic justice and organizational neuroscience. *Journal of Business Ethics, 144*, 733–754.

Curtin, S. C., & Heron, M. (2019, October). *Death rates due to suicide and homicide among persons aged 10–24: United States, 2000–2017.* Accessed at www.cdc.gov/nchs /data/databriefs/db352-h.pdf on May 10, 2021.

Custalow, L., & Daniel, A. L. (2007). *The true story of Pocahontas: The other side of history.* Golden, CO: Fulcrum.

Daley, S. G., & Rappolt-Schlichtmann, G. (2018). *Stigma consciousness among adolescents with learning disabilities: Considering individual experiences of being stereotyped.* Accessed at https://journals.sagepub.com/doi/full/10.1177/0731948718785565 on September 8, 2021.

Davis, J. (2020, June 25). *The bias against difference: And how it gets in the way of creativity and collaboration* [Blog post]. Accessed at www.psychologytoday.com/us/blog /tracking-wonder/202006/the-bias-against-difference on September 14, 2021.

De Lissovoy, N. (2008). *Power, crisis, and education for liberation: Rethinking critical pedagogy.* New York: Palgrave Macmillan.

DiAngelo, R. (2011). White fragility. *International Journal of Critical Pedagogy, 3*(3), 54–70.

DiAngelo, R. (2019). *White people assume niceness is the answer to racial inequality. It's not.* Accessed at www.theguardian.com/commentisfree/2019/jan/16/racial-inequality-niceness-white-people on May 10, 2021.

Dimock, M., & Wike, R. (2020, November 13). *America is exceptional in the nature of its political divide.* Accessed at www.pewresearch.org/fact-tank/2020/11/13/america-is-exceptional-in-the-nature-of-its-political-divide/ on July 27, 2021.

Durlak, J. A., & Mahoney, J. L. (2019). *The practical benefits of an SEL program.* Accessed at https://casel.org/wp-content/uploads/2019/12/Practical-Benefits-of-SEL-Program.pdf on May 10, 2021.

Edwards, G. S., & Rushin, S. (2018). *The effect of President Trump's election on hate crimes.* Accessed at http://dx.doi.org/10.2139/ssrn.3102652 on May 10, 2021.

Emotional intelligence. (n.d.). In *Lexico online dictionary.* Accessed at www.lexico.com/en/definition/emotional_intelligence on September 8, 2021.

Ermolaeva, K. (2019, October 30). *Dinah, put down your horn: Blackface minstrel songs don't belong in music class.* Accessed at https://gen.medium.com/dinah-put-down-your-horn-154b8d8db12a on June 10, 2021.

Eschert, S., & Simon, B. (2019). Respect and political disagreement: Can intergroup respect reduce the biased evaluation of outgroup arguments? *PLOS ONE, 14*(3). Accessed at https://doi.org/10.1371/journal.pone.0211556 on September 14, 2021.

Exploring Your Mind. (2018). *Stress and personal space—When people invade your privacy.* Accessed at https://exploringyourmind.com/stress-and-personal-space-when-people-invade-your-privacy on May 11, 2021.

Farizan, S. (2013). *If you could be mine.* Chapel Hill, NC: Algonquin Young Readers.

Fasciano, M. (2015). *Agree to (respectfully) disagree: How to teach students to respectfully engage with peers of differing religious belief systems.* Accessed at www.tolerance.org/magazine/agree-to-respectfully-disagree on May 10, 2021.

Fink, L. (2017, September 27). *Students have a right and a need to read diverse books* [Blog post]. Accessed at https://ncte.org/blog/2017/09/students-right-need-read-diverse-books on May 10, 2021.

Foley, M., & Graff, C. S. (2018, July 20). *Getting started with person-first language.* Accessed at www.edutopia.org/article/getting-started-person-first-language on June 30, 2021.

Fraley, L. H. (n.d.). *Invisible disabilities—Why they're challenging and how to turn them into superpowers.* Accessed at www.heysigmund.com/invisible-disabilities-theyre-challenging-turn-superpowers-dr-lynn-fraley on May 10, 2021.

Franzosa, S. D. (1993). Shaking the foundations: How schools shortchange girls. *NWSA Journal, 5*(3), 325–339. Accessed at www.jstor.org/stable/4316280 on September 20, 2020.

Friedman, H. H. (2017). Cognitive biases that interfere with critical thinking and scientific reasoning: A course module. *SSRN*. Accessed at https://papers.ssrn .com/sol3/papers.cfm?abstract_id=2958800 on September 14, 2021.

Gal, S., Kiersz, A., Mark, M., Su, R., & Ward, M. (2020, July 8). *26 simple charts to show friends and family who aren't convinced racism is still a problem in America*. Accessed at www.businessinsider.com/us-systemic-racism-in-charts-graphs-data-2020-6 on July 9, 2021.

Gassam, J. (2020). *Dirty diversity: A practical guide to foster an equitable and inclusive workplace for all*. New York: BWG Business Solutions.

Gay and Lesbian Alliance Against Defamation. (n.d.). *GLAAD media reference guide: Lesbian/gay/bisexual glossary of terms*. Accessed at www.glaad.org/reference/lgbtq on September 10, 2021.

Geez, K. (2020). *How to make a bully resign—Advice from a former bully* [Video file]. TED Conferences. Accessed at www.ted.com/talks/kristen_geez_how_to_make_a _bully_resign_advice_from_a_former_bully on May 10, 2021.

Godsil, R. D., Tropp, L. R., Goff, P. A., & powell, j. a. (2014). *Addressing implicit bias, racial anxiety, and stereotype threat in education and health care*. New York: Perception Institute. Accessed at https://perception.org/wp-content/uploads/2014/11/Science -of-Equality.pdf on July 9, 2021.

Goff, P. A., Jackson, M. C., Di Leone, B. A. L., Culotta, C. M., & DiTomasso, N. A. (2014). The essence of innocence: Consequences of dehumanizing Black children. *Journal of Personality and Social Psychology, 106*(4), 526–545. Accessed at www.apa .org/pubs/journals/releases/psp-a0035663.pdf on May 10, 2021.

Gonzalez, M., & SG, M. (2019). *They, she, he easy as ABC*. San Francisco: Reflection Press.

Gonzalez, S. (2020). *Harry Styles wears a dress for* Vogue—*and it's controversial*. Accessed at www.9news.com/article/news/local/mile-high-mornings/harry-styles-wears-dress -vogue-controversial/73-0b7cf24c-c6be-4e6f-a839-ad51a07a01f8 on May 10, 2021.

Gourneau, B. (2005). Five attitudes of effective teachers: Implications for teacher training. *Essays in Education, 13*(5). Accessed at https://openriver.winona.edu/eie/vol13/iss1/5 on May 10, 2021.

Graf, N., Fry, R., & Funk, C. (2018, January 9). *7 facts about the STEM workforce*. Accessed at https://medium.com/@pewresearch/7-facts-about-the-stem-workforce -fe2a9fb87cad on September 2, 2018.

Gramlich, J. (2019, April 30). *The gap between the number of Blacks and Whites in prison is shrinking*. Accessed at www.pewresearch.org/fact-tank/2019/04/30/shrinking-gap -between-number-of-blacks-and-whites-in-prison on May 10, 2021.

Grissom, J. A., & Redding, C. (2016). Discretion and disproportionality: Explaining the underrepresentation of high-achieving students of color in gifted programs. *AERA Open, 2*(1), 1–25. Accessed at https://doi.org/10.1177/2332858415622175 on May 10, 2021.

Harris, T. M., Janovec, A., Murray, S., Gubbala, S., & Robinson, A. (2019). Communicating racism: A study of racial microaggressions in a southern university and the local community. *Southern Communication Journal, 84*(2), 72–84. Accessed at https://doi.org/10.1080/1041794X.2018.1492008 on May 10, 2021.

Herthel, J., & Jennings, J. (2014). *I am Jazz* (S. McNicholas, Illus.). New York: Penguin.

Hofhuis, J., van der Rijt, P. G. A., & Vlug, M. (2016). Diversity climate enhances work outcomes through trust and openness in workgroup communication. *SpringerPlus, 5*(714). Accessed at https://springerplus.springeropen.com/articles/10.1186/s40064 -016-2499-4 on May 10, 2021.

Human Rights Campaign. (2018). *A workplace divided: Understanding the climate for LGBTQ workers nationwide.* Washington DC: Author. Accessed at https://hrc-prod -requests.s3-us-west-2.amazonaws.com/files/assets/resources/AWorkplaceDivided -2018.pdf?mtime=20200713131850&focal=none on September 10, 2021.

Iyer, A., Schmader, T., & Lickel, B. (2007). Why individuals protest the perceived transgressions of their country: The role of anger, shame, and guilt. *Personality and Social Psychology Bulletin, 33*(4), 572–587. Accessed at https://doi. org/10.1177/0146167206297402 on May 10, 2021.

Jackson-Lowman, H. (2014). *An analysis of the impact of Eurocentric concepts of beauty on the lives of Afrikan American women.* Accessed at www.researchgate.net /publication/277709452_An_Analysis_of_the_Impact_of_Eurocentric_Concepts _of_Beauty_on_the_Lives_of_Afrikan_American_Women on May 10, 2021.

Jain, A. (2019, December 20). *Ethics in AI—Responsibilities for data analysts—Part 2 (bias and fairness).* Accessed at https://medium.com/ibm-watson/ethics-in-ai -responsibilities-for-data-analysts-part-2-d76f2343e4d1 on May 10, 2021.

Jennings, J. (2016). *Being Jazz: My life as a (transgender) teen.* New York: Penguin.

Johns Hopkins University. (n.d.). *LGBTQ glossary.* Accessed at https://studentaffairs.jhu .edu/lgbtq/education/glossary on May 10, 2021.

Johnson, J. W. (n.d.). *Lift every voice and sing.* Accessed at www.poetryfoundation.org /poems/46549/lift-every-voice-and-sing on June 9, 2021.

Johnson, T. R., III. (2014, May 11). *Recall that ice cream truck song? We have unpleasant news for you.* Accessed at www.npr.org/sections/codeswitch/2014/05/11/310708342 /recall-that-ice-cream-truck-song-we-have-unpleasant-news-for-you on May 10, 2021.

Jones-Smith, E. (2019). *Culturally diverse counseling: Theory and practice.* Thousand Oaks, CA: SAGE.

Kaltenbach, C. (2015). *Messy grace: How a pastor with gay parents learned to love others without sacrificing conviction.* Colorado Springs, CO: WaterBrook Press.

Kendi, I. X. (2019). *How to be an antiracist.* New York: One World.

Keyes, A. (2010, March 22). *Keep your hands off the hair.* Accessed at www.npr.org /templates/story/story.php?storyId=125020162 on September 14, 2021.

Kimble, L. (2016, June 16). *Michelle Obama loves watching "swagalicious" Barack Obama walk*. Accessed at https://people.com/celebrity/michelle-obama-loves-watching -swagalicious-barack-obama-walk/ on September 14, 2021.

Kirby, R. S. (2017). The U.S. Black-White infant mortality gap: Marker of deep inequities. *American Journal of Public Health, 107*(5), 644–645. Accessed at https:// doi.org/10.2105/AJPH.2017.303735 on May 10, 2021.

Kirwan Institute for the Study of Race and Ethnicity. (2012). *Understanding implicit bias*. Accessed at https://kirwaninstitute.osu.edu/article/understanding-implicit-bias on July 9, 2021.

Kish, S. (2020, August 17). *Language may undermine women in science and tech*. Accessed at www.cmu.edu/news/stories/archives/2020/august/language-may-undermine -women-in-stem.html on September 14, 2021.

Knoester, M., & Au, W. (2017). Standardized testing and school segregation: Like tinder for fire? *Race Ethnicity and Education, 20*(1). Accessed at www.tandfonline.com/doi /full/10.1080/13613324.2015.1121474 on July 1, 2021.

Kosciw, J. G., Palmer, N. A., Kull, R. M., & Greytak, E. A. (2013). The effect of negative school climate on academic outcomes for LGBT youth and the role of in-school supports. *Journal of School Violence, 12*(1), 45–63.

Krulwich, R. (2016, August 26). *Non! Nein! No! A country that wouldn't let women vote till 1971*. Accessed at www.nationalgeographic.com/culture/article/country-that-didnt -let-women-vote-till-1971 on September 13, 2021.

Lawrence-Wilkes, L., & Ashmore, L. (2014) *The reflective practitioner in professional education*. New York: Palgrave Macmillan.

Learning for Justice. (n.d.). *Test yourself for hidden bias*. Accessed at https://bit.ly/3ifrJg3 on June 29, 2021.

Leveridge, A. N. (2008, September). *The relationship between language and culture and the implications for language teaching*. Accessed at www.tefl.net/elt/articles/teacher -technique/language-culture/ on September 9, 2021.

Lewis, M., & Lupyan, G. (2020). Gender stereotypes are reflected in the distributional structure of 25 languages. *Nature Human Behavior, 4*(10), 1021–1028.

LGBT Foundation. (n.d.). *Non-binary inclusion*. Accessed at https://lgbt.foundation/who -we-help/trans-people/non-binary on May 11, 2021.

Lichtblau, E. (2016, September 17). *Hate crimes against American Muslims most since post- 9/11 era*. Accessed at www.nytimes.com/2016/09/18/us/politics/hate-crimes -american-muslims-rise.html on September 14, 2021.

Liebrecht, C., Hustinx, L., & van Mulken, M. (2019). The relative power of negativity: The influence of language intensity on perceived strength. *Journal of Language and Social Psychology, 38*(2), 170–193. Accessed at https://doi.org/10.1177/0261927X18808562 on May 10, 2021.

Limbong, A. (2020, June 9). *Microaggressions are a big deal: How to talk them out and when to walk away*. Accessed at www.npr.org/2020/06/08/872371063 /microaggressions-are-a-big-deal-how-to-talk-them-out-and-when-to-walk-away on May 10, 2021.

Liou, D. D., Marsh, T. E. J., & Antrop-Gonzalez, R. (2016). The spatiality of schooling: A quest for equitable classrooms and high expectations for low-income students of color. *InterActions: UCLA Journal of Education and Information Studies, 12*(2). Accessed at https://escholarship.org/uc/item/4mn4927d on May 10, 2021.

Lorusso L., (2011). The justification of race in biological explanation. *Journal of Medical Ethics, 37*, 535–539. Accessed at https://jme.bmj.com/content/37/9/535.full on May 10, 2021.

Love Has No Labels. (n.d.). *Homepage*. Accessed at https://lovehasnolabels.com/ on November 1, 2021.

Love, J. (2018). *Julián is a mermaid* (J. Love, Illus.). Somerville, MA: Candlewick Press.

Luhmann, N. (1988). Familiarity, confidence, trust: Problems and alternatives. In D. Gambetta (Ed.), *Trust: Making and breaking cooperative relations* (pp. 94–107). Oxford, UK: Basil Blackwell.

Luippold, B. L., Perreault, S., & Wainberg, J. (2015). *Auditors' pitfall: Five ways to overcome confirmation bias*. Accessed at www.babson.edu/academics/executive -education/babson-insight/finance-and-accounting/auditors-pitfall-five-ways-to -overcome-confirmation-bias/# on May 10, 2021.

Making Caring Common Project. (2018). *5 tips for cultivating empathy*. Accessed at https://mcc.gse.harvard.edu/resources-for-families/5-tips-cultivating-empathy on May 10, 2021.

Maslow, A. H. (1987). *Motivation and personality* (3rd ed.). New York: Harper & Row.

Math and Social Justice: A Collaborative MTBoS Site. (n.d.). *Curriculum resources*. Accessed at https://sites.google.com/site/mathandsocialjustice/curriculum-resources on May 10, 2021.

McAvoy, P. (2016). *Polarized classrooms: Understanding political divides can help students learn to bridge them*. Accessed at www.tolerance.org/magazine/fall-2016/polarized -classrooms on May 10, 2021.

McCluney, C. L., Robotham, K., Lee, S., Smith, R., & Durkee, M. (2019, November 15). *The costs of code-switching*. Accessed at https://hbr.org/2019/11/the-costs-of -codeswitching on May 10, 2021.

Miceli, M., & Castelfranchi, C. (2018). Reconsidering the differences between shame and guilt. *Europe's Journal of Psychology, 14*(3), 710–733. Accessed at https://doi .org/10.5964/ejop.v14i3.1564 on May 10, 2021.

Microaggression. (n.d.). In *Lexico online dictionary*. Accessed at www.lexico.com/en /definition/microaggression on September 13, 2021.

Miller, S. (2021, February 24). *'Society is changing': A record 5.6% of US adults identify as LGBTQ, poll shows. And young people are driving the numbers*. Accessed at www

.usatoday.com/story/news/nation/2021/02/24/lgbtq-gallup-poll-more-us-adults -identify-lgbtq/4532664001/ on September 14, 2021.

Minero, E. (2018, April 19). *Schools struggle to support LGBTQ students: Recent research finds the majority of teachers want to help LGBTQ students but don't always know how.* Accessed at www.edutopia.org/article/schools-struggle-support-lgbtq-students on September 14, 2021.

Mitchell, R. (2019, February 15). *How to navigate the gender landscape at work.* Accessed at https://news.harvard.edu/gazette/story/2019/02/lessons-in-how-to-make-the -workplace-inclusive-for-lgbtq-employees on May 10, 2021.

Mitchell-Yellin, B. (2019, September 27). *Righting the wrongs of erasure: Why we have ethical reasons to revise the dominant historical narrative.* Accessed at www .psychologytoday.com/us/blog/life-death-and-the-self/201909/righting-the-wrongs -erasure on September 14, 2021.

Montz, B. (2019, August 12). *Acronyms explained.* Accessed at https:// outrightinternational.org/content/acronyms-explained on July 9, 2021.

Movement Advancement Project. (n.d.). *Nondiscrimination laws.* Accessed at www .lgbtmap.org/equality-maps/non_discrimination_laws on May 11, 2021.

Nadal, K. (2018). *Microaggressions and traumatic stress: Theory, research, and clinical treatment.* Washington, DC: American Psychological Association. Accessed at www .apa.org/pubs/books/Microaggressions-and-Traumatic-Stress-Series-Forward-and -Intro-Sample.pdf on September 14, 2021.

Nadal, K. L., Erazo, T., & King, R. (2019). Challenging definitions of psychological trauma: Connecting racial microaggressions and traumatic stress. *Journal for Social Action in Counseling and Psychology, 11*(2), 2–16.

National Alliance on Mental Illness. (n.d.). *LGBTQI.* Accessed at www.nami.org/Your -Journey/Identity-and-Cultural-Dimensions/LGBTQI on September 10, 2021.

National Center for Science and Engineering Statistics. (2021). *Women, minorities, and persons with disabilities in science and engineering.* Accessed at https://ncses.nsf.gov /pubs/nsf21321 on July 9, 2021.

National Hispanic Heritage Month. (n.d.). *About National Hispanic Heritage Month.* Accessed at www.hispanicheritagemonth.gov/about/ on September 13, 2021.

Newport, F. (2018, May 22). *In U.S., estimate of LGBT population rises to 4.5%.* Accessed at https://news.gallup.com/poll/234863/estimate-lgbt-population-rises.aspx on September 26, 2020.

Nichols, H. (2021). *What is anti-racism?* Ann Arbor, MI: Cherry Lake.

Noor, I. (2020). *Confirmation bias.* Accessed at www.simplypsychology.org/confirmation -bias.html on May 11, 2021.

Oakes, A. (2013). *Family-school partnerships: 9 beliefs and attitudes for success.* Accessed at www.studentachievement.org/blog/9-beliefs-and-attitudes-that-foster-collaborative -family-school-partnerships on May 10, 2021.

Ogle, D. (1986). K-W-L: A teaching model that develops active reading of expository text. *The Reading Teacher, 39*(6), 564–570.

Oppelt, J. S. (2012). *15 great principles shared by all religions.* Accessed at https:// integralchurch.wordpress.com/2012/07/10/15-great-principles-shared-by-all-religions on May 11, 2021.

Osborne, M. (2018, December 22). *Racial bias investigation launched after high school wrestler forced to cut off dreadlocks.* Accessed at https://abcnews.go.com/US/racial-bias -investigation-launched-high-school-wrestler-forced/story?id=59969333 on September 14, 2021.

PBS. (2002). *Citizen Ben: Abolitionist.* Accessed at www.pbs.org/benfranklin/l3_citizen _abolitionist.html on September 9, 2021.

Pentecost, J. (Producer), Gabriel, M. (Director), & Goldberg, E. (Director). (1995). *Pocahontas* [Motion picture]. United States: Walt Disney Pictures.

Powell, A. (2016, December 9). *The everyday response to racism.* Accessed at news.harvard .edu/gazette/story/2016/12/the-everyday-response-to-racism on May 11, 2021.

Prager, S. (2017). *Queer, there, and everywhere: 23 people who changed the world* (Z. M. O'Ferrall, Illus.). New York: HarperCollins.

Project Implicit. (n.d.). *About us.* Accessed at https://implicit.harvard.edu/implicit /aboutus.html on May 10, 2021.

Reneau, A. (2020, June 25). *Childhood nursery rhymes and other "classic" songs you probably never knew were racist.* Accessed at www.upworthy.com/racist-nursery-rhymes-and -songs on June 10, 2021.

Richards, J. C., & Bennett, S. M. (2013). *Devising and investigating benefits of interconnected interventions to promote education majors' culturally responsive teaching.* Accessed at www.academia.edu/5112235/Running_head_CULTURALLY _RESPONSIVE_TEACHING_Devising_and_Investigating_Benefits_of _Interconnected_Interventions_to_Promote_Education_Majors_Culturally _Responsive_Teaching on May 11, 2021.

Richardson, J., & Parnell, P. (2005). *And Tango makes three* (H. Cole, Illus.). New York: Simon & Schuster Books for Young Readers.

Riddle, T., & Sinclair, S. (2019). *Racial disparities in school-based disciplinary actions are associated with county-level rates of racial bias.* Accessed at www.pnas.org /content/116/17/8255 on August 18, 2020.

Robinson, J. P., & Espelage, D. L. (2012). Bullying explains only part of LGBTQ— heterosexual risk disparities: Implications for policy and practice. *Educational Researcher, 41*(8), 309–319. Accessed at www.jstor.org/stable/23272324 on December 30, 2020.

Rodriguez, A. (n.d.). *White fragility, guilt, and unvirtuous virtue: The damaging effects of power and privilege, part III* [Blog post]. Accessed at www.psychedinsanfrancisco .com/white-fragility-guilt-privilege on May 11, 2021.

Rorby, G. (2019). *Freeing Finch*. New York: Tom Doherty Associates.

Salter, M. (2018). From geek masculinity to Gamergate: The technological rationality of online abuse. *Crime, Media, Culture: An International Journal, 14*(2), 247–264. Accessed at https://doi.org/10.1177/1741659017690893 on May 10, 2021.

Sankofa, B. M., Hurley, E. A., Allen, B. A., & Boykin, A. W. (2005). Cultural expression and black students' attitudes toward high achievers. *The Journal of Psychology, 139*(3), 247–260. Accessed at https://doi.org/10.3200/JRLP.139.3.247-260 on May 10, 2021.

Schlanger, Z. (2015, October 5). *Company apologizes for Texas textbook calling slaves "workers": "We made a mistake."* Accessed at www.newsweek.com/company-behind -texas-textbook-calling-slaves-workers-apologizes-we-made-380168 on September 14, 2021.

Schmitt, G. R., Reedt, L., & Blackwell, K. (2017). *Demographic differences in sentencing: An update to the 2012* Booker *Report*. Accessed at www.ussc.gov/sites/default/files /pdf/research-and-publications/research-publications/2017/20171114_Demographics .pdf on July 9, 2021.

Scott, D. M. (2011). *Origins of black history month*. Accessed at https://asalh.org/about-us /origins-of-black-history-month on May 11, 2021.

Segal, E. (2011). Social empathy: A model built on empathy, contextual understanding, and social responsibility that promotes social justice. *Journal of Social Service Research, 37*(3), 266–277. Accessed at https://doi.org/10.1080/01488376.2011.564040 on September 14, 2021.

Seidman, G. (2018, December 18). *Why do we like people who are similar to us?* [Blog post]. Accessed at www.psychologytoday.com/us/blog/close-encounters/201812/why -do-we-people-who-are-similar-us on May 11, 2021.

Shen, D. (n.d.). *Debate*. Accessed at https://ablconnect.harvard.edu/debate-research on May 11, 2021.

Shernoff, D. J., Ruzek, E. A., & Sinha, S. (2017). The influence of the high school classroom environment on learning as mediated by student engagement. *School Psychology International, 38*(2), 201–218. Accessed at https://doi .org/10.1177/0143034316666413 on May 11, 2021.

Silvera, A. (2015). *More happy than not*. New York: Soho Teen.

Sjöblom, M., Öhrling, K., & Kostenius, C. (2018). Useful life lessons for health and well-being: Adults' reflections of childhood experiences illuminate the phenomenon of the inner child. *International Journal of Qualitative Studies on Health and Well-being, 13*(1). Accessed at https://doi.org/10.1080/17482631.2018.1441592 on May 11, 2021.

Solano-Flores, G. (2006). Language, dialect, and register: Sociolinguistics and the estimation of measurement error in the testing of English language learners. *Teachers College Record, 108*(11), 2354–2379.

Sparks, S. D. (2019, March 12). *Why teacher-student relationships matter*. Accessed at www.edweek.org/teaching-learning/why-teacher-student-relationships-matter/2019/03 on July 7, 2021.

Spencer, E. A., & Heneghan, C. (2018). *Confirmation bias*. Accessed at https://catalogofbias.org/biases/confirmation-bias/ on May 10, 2021.

Stanford History Education Group. (n.d.). *Multiperspectivity: What is it, and why use it?* Accessed at teachinghistory.org/teaching-materials/ask-a-master-teacher/23610 on May 11, 2021.

Starr, D. (2020, March 26). *Meet the psychologist exploring unconscious bias—and its tragic consequences for society*. Accessed at www.sciencemag.org/news/2020/03/meet-psychologist-exploring-unconscious-bias-and-its-tragic-consequences-society on May 11, 2021.

Sue, D. W. (2010, October 5). *Racial microaggressions in everyday life* [Blog post]. Accessed at www.psychologytoday.com/us/blog/microaggressions-in-everyday-life/201010/racial-microaggressions-in-everyday-life on May 11, 2021.

Sugar, R. (Executive Producer). (2013–2019). *Steven Universe* [TV Series]. Cartoon Network Studios.

Tatum, B. (1992). Talking about race, learning about racism: The application of racial identity development theory in the classroom. *Harvard Educational Review*, *62*(1), 1–25. Accessed at https://doi.org/10.17763/haer.62.1.146k5v980r703023 on May 11, 2021.

Teroni, F., & Bruun, O. (2011). Shame, guilt and morality. *Journal of Moral Philosophy*, *8*(2), 223–245. Accessed at https://doi.org/10.1163/174552411X563574 on May 11, 2021.

Thomas, A. (2017). *The hate u give*. New York: Balzer + Bray.

Thomas, R. (2018, March 14). *Oldest school desegregation case in La. finally resolved*. Accessed at www.wafb.com/story/37727803/oldest-school-desegregation-case-in-la-finally-resolved/ on September 13, 2021.

Thomas, W. I., & Thomas, D. S. (1928). *The child in America: Behavior problems and programs*. New York: Knopf.

Thorn, T. (2019). *It feels good to be yourself: A book about gender identity* (N. Grigni, Illus.). New York: Holt.

Trevor Project. (n.d.). *Glossary: Key terms*. Accessed at www.thetrevorproject.org/trvr_support_center/glossary/ on September 10, 2021.

Trevor Project. (2021, March 11). *Estimate of how often LGBTQ youth attempt suicide in the U.S.* Accessed at www.thetrevorproject.org/2021/03/11/estimate-of-how-often-lgbtq-youth-attempt-suicide-in-the-u-s/ on September 10, 2021.

Turnbull, B., & Evans, M. S. (2017). The effects of L1 and L2 group discussions on L2 reading comprehension. *Reading in a Foreign Language*, *29*(1), 133–154.

United States Census Bureau. (2018, March 19). *United States population projections: 2000 to 2050*. Accessed at www.census.gov/library/working-papers/2009/demo/us-pop-proj-2000-2050.html on September 14, 2021.

United States Department of Education. (2016). *The state of racial diversity in the educator workforce.* Accessed at www2.ed.gov/rschstat/eval/highered/racial-diversity/state -racial-diversity-workforce.pdf on May 10, 2021.

United States Department of Justice. (2015, August 6). *Combating post-9/11 discriminatory backlash.* Accessed at www.justice.gov/crt/combating-post-911-discriminatory -backlash-6 on May 10, 2021.

United States Government Accountability Office. (2018). *K–12 education: Discipline disparities for Black students, boys, and students with disabilities.* Accessed at www.gao .gov/products/gao-18-258 on May 11, 2021.

United States Sentencing Commission. (n.d.). *Demographic differences in sentencing.* Accessed at www.ussc.gov/research/research-reports/demographic-differences -sentencing on September 14, 2021.

University of California San Francisco Lesbian, Gay, Bisexual and Transgender Resource Center. (n.d.). *General definitions.* Accessed at https://lgbt.ucsf.edu/glossary -terms#:~:text=Sexuality on May 10, 2021.

Walton, J. (2016). *Introducing Teddy: A gentle story about gender and friendship* (D. MacPherson, Illus.). New York: Bloomsbury.

Wamsley, L. (2018, December 27). *Adults come under scrutiny after HS wrestler told to cut his dreadlocks or forfeit.* Accessed at www.npr.org/2018/12/27/680470933/after -h-s-wrestler-told-to-cut-his-dreadlocks-or-forfeit-adults-come-under-scrut on June 9, 2021.

Welsh, R. O., & Little, S. (2018). The school discipline dilemma: A comprehensive review of disparities and alternative approaches. *Review of Educational Research, 88*(5), 752– 794. Accessed at https://doi.org/10.3102/0034654318791582 on May 11, 2021.

White, J. W., & Ali-Khan, C. (2013). The role of academic discourse in minority students' academic assimilation. *American Secondary Education, 42*(1), 24–42. Accessed at www.jstor.org/stable/43694175 on August 12, 2020.

Williams, K. L., Coles, J. A., & Reynolds, P. (2020). (Re)creating the script: A framework of agency, accountability, and resisting deficit depictions of Black students in P-20 education. *The Journal of Negro Education, 89*(3), 249–266. Accessed at www.jstor .org/stable/10.7709/jnegroeducation.89.3.0249 on May 11, 2021.

Index

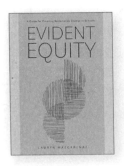

Evident Equity
Lauryn Mascareñaz

Make equity the norm in your school or district. *Evident Equity* provides a comprehensive method that leaders can use to integrate equitable practices into every facet of their school communities and offers real-life examples at the elementary, middle, and high school levels.

BKG032

Beyond Conversations About Race
Washington Collado, Sharroky Hollie, Rosa Isiah, Yvette Jackson, Anthony Muhammad, Douglas Reeves, and Kenneth C. Williams

Written by a collective of brilliant authors, this essential work provokes respectful dialogue about race that catalyzes school-changing action. The book masterfully weaves together an array of scenarios, discussions, and challenging topics to help prepare all of us to do better in our schools and communities.

BKG035

Dismantling a Broken System
Zachary Wright

Become a hyperlocal activist for change and help ensure a bright future for every student. Written for educators at all levels, this resource dives into the American education system, exposing the history of discrimination and offering strategies for establishing financially and academically equitable learning environments.

BKG015

Supporting Underserved Students
Sharroky Hollie and Daniel Russell, Jr.

Discover a clear two-step roadmap for aligning PBIS with culturally and linguistically responsive teaching. First, you'll dive deep into why there is an urgent need for this alignment and then learn how to move forward to better serve all learners, especially those from historically underserved populations.

BKG010

Solution Tree | Press
a division of
Solution Tree

Visit SolutionTree.com or call 800.733.6786 to order.

Wait! Your professional development journey doesn't have to end with the last pages of this book.

We realize improving student learning doesn't happen overnight. And your school or district shouldn't be left to puzzle out all the details of this process alone.

No matter where you are on the journey, we're committed to helping you get to the next stage.

Take advantage of everything from **custom workshops** to **keynote presentations** and **interactive web and video conferencing**. We can even help you develop an action plan tailored to fit your specific needs.

Let's get the conversation started.

Call 888.763.9045 today.

SolutionTree.com